NEVER STOP DREAMING

MY EURO 96 STORY

STUART PEARCE

HODDER

First published in Great Britain in 2020 by Hodder & Stoughton
An Hachette UK company

1

Copyright © Stuart Pearce 2020

A CIP catalogue record for this title is available from the British Library

Hardback ISBN 978 1 529 34854 5
eBook ISBN 978 1 529 34856 9

Typeset in Adobe Caslon Pro by Hewer Text UK Ltd, Edinburgh

Printed and bound in Great Britain by Clays Ltd, Elcograf S.p.A.

Hodder & Stoughton policy is to use papers that are natural, renewable and recyclable
products and made from wood grown in sustainable forests. The logging and manufacturing
processes are expected to conform to the environmental regulations of the country of origin.

Hodder & Stoughton Ltd
Carmelite House
50 Victoria Embankment
London EC4Y 0DZ

www.hodder.co.uk

*For Carol, and for the players, staff and supporters
who made Euro 96 such a special time.*

ACKNOWLEDGEMENTS

I would particularly like to thank Oliver Holt for carefully listening to my story, and then helping me to shape the words so well. Many thanks also to Hodder & Stoughton, my publishers, for the many hours they have spent in the course of producing this fine-looking book.

CONTENTS

PROLOGUE

FOOTBALL WAS ALWAYS what I wanted to do. I played for two decades in the professional game and when someone asks me what was the most important thing I won, I always say an England cap. Individual medals didn't matter so much. Playing for England was the pinnacle of my career and every cap carried the same weight for me.

But there was one experience of playing for my country that I loved more than any other. That was playing for England in the 1996 European Championship. It is a rare honour to play for your country in a home tournament, to be at the core of all the hope and patriotism and unity that floods through the nation, and that was what it was like to be an England player at Euro 96.

So many things came together for me at that tournament. I was 34 by the time it began, so I always knew it was likely to be my last hurrah on the biggest stage and I savoured every minute of it. I rode my luck a bit in terms of keeping my place in the side, but I started every one of our five games and surfed the wave of emotion all the way.

I wasn't actively seeking redemption for missing the critical penalty in the shoot-out at the end of the 1990 World Cup semi-final against West Germany, but redemption found me anyway. It found me at the end of the Euro 96 quarter-final against Spain, when there was another penalty shoot-out and I took another penalty.

It found other people in that side, too. Paul Gascoigne had been ridiculed and pilloried by the press before the tournament, but he emerged from it, just as he had in 1990, as a national hero. Alan Shearer was surrounded by doubts before the tournament and he finished it with the Golden Boot. Tony Adams was facing personal demons but he was a lion of a captain.

It took a little longer for Gareth Southgate to find his redemption, not that he had anything to be ashamed of. But when he took England to the World Cup in 2018 as manager and led them to their best performance in a generation, uniting the country in the process, his football life came full circle.

There were wider issues at Euro 96, too, that made it special to be a part of. Our success in the tournament seemed to create a moment of national catharsis. Sixteen years before the London Olympics, it was an event which allowed us to feel good about ourselves for a little while and abandon ourselves to a happy kind of patriotism unlike the brand our football supporters sometimes took abroad.

I played on for a while after those Euros but, in a way, that tournament defined me. It cemented my reputation among the supporters as one of them, I think. It underlined my image as someone who would give everything for their country, because people could see it written on my face. Some people pay lip service to being proud to represent their country, but I don't pay lip service. I was a hard-nosed bastard, someone that people liked to call 'Psycho', but playing for England was at my core.

*   *   *

I'm not sure I'm a psycho but I did want to give everything and I never wanted to show I was hurt. I suppose that came from my upbringing. My parents were married for fifty years and so I had a really stable background. My eldest brother, who is fifteen years older than me, was into football and boxed at amateur level and he was like an auxiliary dad to me.

My old man was there for pretty much every football match I ever played as a kid. He used to work in hotels and restaurants in London as a head waiter, places like The Savoy and Quaglino's. He got us out of Shepherd's Bush, which was a bit rough at the time, and we moved out to Kingsbury, in north-west London, which was a nicer area but more expensive, so he had to get a decent mortgage.

He didn't drive because he had no patience, so my mum drove him to central London to go to work in the morning and then picked him up from work in the early hours. He did that every day until he had paid the mortgage off. The day he got the money for the final payment, he packed his job in.

He got a job in the local post office that finished at 1 p.m., so he could come and watch me play school football, district football, county football or whatever. I always knew he was there when he was on the touchline, but he wouldn't say a word. He just gave me a look.

It was always pumped into me to never let the opposition see you were hurt. Some of that probably came from my eldest brother being a boxer, too. If you show any vulnerability in a boxing ring, you are in big trouble. It makes the opposition come on to you. The old man was similar with me. *Never show the opposition you are hurt. If you are hurt, get up.* That was drummed into me.

All of a sudden, twenty-five years later, I am playing for West Ham and I break my shin and I get up and walk off – because of his words. That was his influence. You get on top of the opposition and you don't show weakness and you grind them down. My parents were fantastic role models to me in terms of values.

I used to put too much into the preparation to get on to the pitch to be rolled over by somebody because I hadn't given my all in terms of determination or I didn't want it enough or didn't have it in my heart.

I fed off anger. That's part of my personality. A refusal to be cowed. Sometimes things happen in games and you get an almost superhuman energy from somewhere. You can't play ninety minutes in a state of rage, of course, but if someone has wronged you in a game, that little burst of energy you get from the anger can turn the tide.

I wasn't stupid. I didn't let rage rule me. If I felt somebody would get the better of me physically, I wouldn't take them on. I wouldn't back away from a challenge or a tackle. But I wouldn't have taken on Mick Harford or John Fashanu, because there would only have been one winner. I wouldn't make it a physical encounter as that plays right into their hands. I had a little bit of know-how about me.

You fight on your terms and use your strongest card. It's like Top Trumps. If I felt I could intimidate someone to make my life easier during a game, then I would do so. If that individual was stronger than me, then, apart from the times when the ball falls between the two of you and there is no backing down, I wouldn't turn it into a physical encounter. Why would you?

I saw something written in the paper the other day and the question was 'Are you motivated more by love or hate when you play football and which is the more powerful?' Interesting question. Really interesting. If it were me, I would lean towards hate.

I remember the former Liverpool defender Neil Ruddock talking about this and he said, 'If I want to play better in a game, I just lose my temper.' You find this extra surge from somewhere. As long as you can control that, you can use it and you can profit from it.

I played with hate for England, too. I played with resentment and anger. I saw criticism coming, so I used the hate as a kind of pre-emptive strike. There was so much hostility from the press, in particular, when you played for your country that it was easy. You tell yourself, 'OK, what have I got to lose?' You are in front of a firing squad anyway, so it doesn't make any difference; you might just as well come out fighting.

At the World Cup in 1990 and at Euro 96, the England players got so sick of the criticism before the competitions had even started that we thought, 'Stuff you, what's the worst that can happen to us now? You've already had a dig at us, you've put a marker down that you don't like us and you think we're rubbish, so we'll just have to show you.' And in both tournaments, we showed them.

At the other end of the spectrum, you do what Gareth did with the England team and the media before the 2018 World Cup and you build the love. His players felt as though the pressure had been taken off them. They felt that the media were right behind them and, more importantly, the crowd and the supporters watching at home were right behind them, too.

At both ends of the spectrum the pressure was taken off. It is the in-between that is the killer when it comes to adversely affecting the players. It's the not knowing whether you are going to be slaughtered or whether you are going to be given the benefit of the doubt. It's the idea that if you make a mistake, there will be people coming for you, but if you do OK, or if you hide, then you might escape.

So I've seen Kieron Dyer, for example, say that he was afraid to take risks for England or play his normal game because he was worried about the reaction of the media or the crowd in the stadium, and I understand that. He was caught between two emotions. He never got to the position where he was entrenched, saying it was him against the world, or where he was loved no matter whether he excelled in a game or not and could grow in stature accordingly.

In my case, I would motivate myself by hating the opposition. It wouldn't be outside influences like the media. It was controlled aggression. My game was built on controlled aggression. There may have been other facets of the game that I wasn't bad at as well, but if you asked supporters what epitomised me, they would say aggression.

I was also cold and calculating. I'm not sure many people saw that. I would do what I could up to the edge of the laws of the game, but I would try not to let the team down by going too far. I would never go over the top and get myself sent off. You have to be quite clinical in your mentality and know how far you can take it and where to draw the line to keep yourself out of trouble with the officials.

That didn't stop me making things personal on the pitch. I had no problem at all doing that. That motivated me. I have played against people who are really good friends and my attitude was that all is fair in love and war. I would give them no quarter and they would expect that.

Trevor Peake was a mate of mine when we played at Coventry and he was the best man at my wedding, but when I was with Nottingham Forest, every time we played against Coventry, if I had a chance to get involved in a challenge with him, I'd take it. He once got so incensed after one of my tackles on him, he chased me halfway up the pitch. Listen, you're wearing a different-coloured shirt to me. That's the beginning and the end of it.

People will bump into me sometimes and we'll have a chat and they'll say, 'I hadn't realised you were such a nice bloke.' I'm not a bad bloke. I think I take a lot of people by surprise. But playing football is about winning. It's about the moment and it's about the game. After the game, it's about being a nice person, or the best person you can possibly be.

I didn't mind being nicknamed 'Psycho'. I took it as a compliment from the fans. It was funny. But it didn't mean I was some sort of madman. When I was a coach at Manchester City, Kevin Keegan signed the Germany international Michael Tarnat and when he arrived at the training ground, I introduced myself. He said, 'Oh, I know you, you're crazy, aren't you?' 'No,' I said. 'No, I'm not.'

I played the game in a certain way, but the stakes were high. I make no apologies for anything I have done on a football pitch. There was a desperation to win and play your strongest card and sometimes my strongest card was aggression and the ability to intimidate an opponent. Don't ask me not to be aggressive on a football pitch. It's like asking Gazza not to play a key pass.

I always liked Pat Nevin but he was on the worst end of a lot of things when we played against each other. It was almost a mark of respect from me. People don't realise it but the players I roughed up the most were the ones I knew I would have to quieten down. If I wasn't worried about a player, if I didn't think he might give me a problem, I wouldn't bother.

If it was Nevin or Matt Le Tissier and I thought, 'Damn, I've got a tough day ahead of me if this fella has a good 'un,' they would get roughed up. If I was up against someone and I thought, 'He's not going to cause me a problem, he can't beat me, he can't run away from me,' I wouldn't waste a booking on him. It's just cold and calculating.

There were times when I thought I wouldn't even make it to Euro 96. I knew that Terry Venables, the England manager, didn't rate me particularly highly and that his first-choice left back was Graeme Le Saux. I knew that age was catching up with me and that some people felt I ought to accept the inevitable, step back and admit defeat.

I didn't want to do that. I didn't want to retire. I wasn't ready. I loved playing for my country, so when Terry gave me the opportunity to go out on my own terms, I declined the invitation. I said I'd take my chances. I knew I was past my best, but I also understood that I knew my craft. And I knew that being involved in Euro 96 was a prize worth fighting for.

After everything that had happened at the 1990 World Cup, and especially that night in Turin, I had a debt to my country that I didn't realise I owed until the afternoon at Wembley when I paid it back.

THE RIGHT STUFF?

I PLAYED SEVENTY-EIGHT TIMES for England over the course of a twelve-year international career. I will be remembered, I think, for the love I had of playing for my country and for two penalties. I missed one and I scored the other. I'm lucky that they came in the right order: the journey towards my defining moment of putting away that penalty against Spain in the quarter-finals of Euro 96 had begun six years earlier on a night of heartbreak in Italy.

When I walked from the centre circle towards the penalty spot at the Stadio delle Alpi in Turin on the night of 4 July 1990, most people thought I was going to score. That was partly because I had established myself as a regular and successful penalty-taker for Nottingham Forest. But it was also because fans thought I was made of the right stuff.

These were the deciding moments of a World Cup semi-final against West Germany, but being made of the right stuff was about as far as the science of penalty-taking went in those days. It was about character. That was how it was seen. There was no inkling that maybe we should be studying the statistics of how successful each player was when practising penalties.

Practising penalties was actively frowned upon by some managers, anyway. Even when I went to the 2010 World Cup as part of Fabio Capello's coaching set-up, it was frowned upon.

Fabio didn't want the players practising penalties and he didn't want the goalkeepers thinking about them, either. He thought it would distract them from the business of the match itself. Penalties were only ever an afterthought.

So when I walked up to the spot in Turin, Martin Tyler, the match commentator, was pleased for those reasons: 'England will feel pretty happy about Stuart Pearce coming up in this situation,' he told the millions watching at home in England as I prepared to take our fourth penalty. 'A man who doesn't mince his words and really doesn't mess about when it comes to hitting a football.'

I had loved everything about my experience at that World Cup until then. It was the first time I had played in a major tournament; I was young and confident; and I was playing for a manager, Sir Bobby Robson, who I respected and who I knew had faith in me. Not many people have a bad word to say about Sir Bobby and I'm the same.

I'm forever indebted to him because he gave me my first international cap. Kenny Sansom was the starting left back before me. He was one of our all-time great defenders and somebody I admired. I was in awe of him, really. When I was a non-league player at Wealdstone, my manager introduced me to Kenny at an awards dinner. He had a bottle of champagne tucked under his arm and when my boss told him I was going to be an England player, too, one day, he was generous in his advice.

Sansom was approaching 30 when he played in the 1988 European Championship, which was a poor tournament for England, and after they were over there was a clamour for me to replace him. Some people in football harboured doubts about my playing style and said that the way I tackled and the aggression I showed would be a problem in the international game, but Sir Bobby ignored them.

I had made my debut in May 1987 in a Rous Cup game against Brazil but I missed out on the Euros because of a knee-ligament injury and so Sir Bobby picked Sansom and Tony Dorigo. After the Euros, though, I became the starting left back and by the time the 1990 World Cup came around, I had already won twenty-four caps. When the tournament began, I felt that I was ready.

There is a lot of nostalgia about Italia 90 now and it is easy to forget that we went into that tournament against a backdrop of concern about English football hooliganism. English clubs were still banned from European competition after the Heysel Stadium disaster of 1985 and there had been problems with our supporters in Germany two years earlier. Some politicians were suggesting that the team should be brought home at the first hint of trouble.

The sports minister, Colin Moynihan, had called our fans 'worse than animals'. Hooliganism still blighted our game and English football was still reeling from the great tragedy of the Hillsborough disaster of 1989. Margaret Thatcher was prime minister and her view of our fans was that they were 'a disgrace to Britain'. It was a view shared by many. We were exiled to Sardinia to play all our group games, away from the Italian mainland.

It was said there were almost 7,000 Italian police in Cagliari for the first match, more than the total of England fans. The supporters who misbehaved were given short shrift by the forces of law and order. Many of them complained of victimisation. Moynihan responded by sending a letter to the Italian government, praising the way they had dealt with the situation. That endeared him to the England fans.

The atmosphere between the players and the media was fraught, too. It was known that Sir Bobby was going to be leaving after the tournament – he had effectively been forced out by the FA – and to the players, the attitude of the press seemed to be that they were ready to give him a kick up the backside to help him on his way. We didn't like that and so there was a stand-off.

It is easy now to think that Sir Bobby was always regarded with great affection by the media and the fans. That was the way it should have been. But it certainly didn't feel that way in Italy. He was mocked and hounded by the press. His tactics were ridiculed and they made him out to be a fool. That was all conveniently forgotten in later years when he was anointed a national treasure.

The pre-tournament camp in Sardinia didn't go particularly smoothly. There was one occasion when I saw Steve McMahon, the Liverpool midfielder, picking up a copy of a tabloid newspaper and ripping it to pieces because there was a false story about some players having a fling with an Italian public relations girl. There was even a suggestion that I was involved at one point. That, at least, gave some of the other players a laugh, but there was definitely a feeling of 'them and us'. In fact, there was a feeling of 'us against the world'.

There was something similar before Euro 96, when there was the furore about the players' behaviour in Hong Kong and the Dentist's Chair incident, but the animosity was worse in 1990. In Italy, the relationship with the media was particularly volatile and hostile, and it had the effect of galvanising the squad.

Paul Parker was just about the only player who would speak to the press in Sardinia. Gazza threw a bottle of water over him at one point during an interview. I didn't give any interviews but that wasn't particularly unusual. A few years earlier, when Sansom was still the first-choice left back, I'd done an article with a reporter who had asked me whether I was looking forward to playing for England. I had said that I was, obviously, but it was made to look as if I was big-headed and that I was expecting to displace Kenny.

I hated that. So I stopped doing interviews. I just didn't want distractions. I didn't want to speak to a paper and tell them a story about myself and then worry about how it had been portrayed. It meant that when I opened up a newspaper, I never needed to worry about the possibility I'd dropped myself in the mire.

I got a reputation as someone who disliked the press, which wasn't really true. It was just self-protection. You get a bit of experience about how the media can work sometimes. I knew that they needed to sell their stories with decent headlines and that worthy sentiments wouldn't be enough for them. So I steered clear as best I could. A few years later, I picked up a paper and saw a picture of Tony Dorigo with the headline 'I want your job, Stuart Pearce'. It made me smile. It was history repeating itself.

* * *

There was pressure on us when we got to Italy. England had reached the quarter-finals of the World Cup four years earlier under Sir Bobby and had come home with a kind of honour after being knocked out by Diego Maradona's brilliance and his handball goal. But the Euros in 1988 had been a disaster and it felt as if some of the media wanted us to fail again.

I enjoyed the build-up to the tournament anyway, but it wasn't without incident. We played a warm-up game in June against Tunisia in Tunis and only managed a draw, which prompted more criticism of the manager. The press had already used up 'In the Name of Allah, Go' as a headline a couple of years earlier, after a game against Saudi Arabia, but now there was another inquest.

And there were fun and games in Sardinia, too. Many felt that that tournament marked a change in the nature of the relationship between the players and the media. Until then, there had been quite a few friendships between the two camps and we would often travel on the same plane to matches. But now there was a different kind of interest in what the players were up to and a lot of the senior professionals felt that it crossed a line. There were news reporters on these trips now, not just the sports reporters we knew. The agenda was changing. It was the beginning of the press prying into the private lives of players.

We were staying at the Is Molas resort 20 miles outside Cagliari and that story about the public relations woman, in particular, had made the players suspect the press were trying to undermine us. Gazza gave an interview where he said it felt as if the press were making it impossible for the players to enjoy being at the World Cup. He said the press were trying to ruin players' lives.

It was known that Sir Bobby would be at PSV Eindhoven the next season and that was another source of tension. One paper accused him of betrayal and said that in former times, he would have been locked up in the Tower of London for treason like that. That was the kind of thing that made other players want to rip up newspapers, too.

The treatment that Bobby Robson got was interesting. When he was with England, he was often lampooned. He was portrayed as an old dodderer who couldn't even get people's names right and who was a victim of player power. He was underestimated and he was patronised. He had never won the league title as a manager, even though he had done fantastic work with Ipswich Town, and so, in some quarters of the press, he was not treated with quite the same seriousness as some other managers.

And yet after he left the England job, everything changed. It wasn't long before people realised quite what they had had in Sir Bobby Robson. They began to recognise the measure of the man they had mocked and understood that maybe they ought to have treated him with a little more respect.

He travelled around Europe as a manager, from Eindhoven to Sporting Lisbon and Porto, and then to the biggest club job of his life, at Barcelona. People didn't mock him any more then. It was then that they said he was a national treasure and realised that he was not only a fine manager but a great man.

He ended his career by managing his home-town club, Newcastle United, and he was so beloved in the north-east that they built a statue of him after he had gone. He got his rewards in the end. He got the respect he deserved. But when we were in Sardinia ahead of the 1990 World Cup, that respect felt a long, long way away.

It wasn't easy for the manager. Sometimes, things seemed to be conspiring against him. Our captain, Bryan Robson, hurt his toe when he tried to tip Steve Hodge off a bed and the bed landed on his foot. Seven players had been for a night out in the local town, Pula, so the rest of us christened them the Pula Seven. Robson needed an injection in his toe to play in the first game, against the Republic of Ireland, and then damaged his Achilles tendon in the second game, against Holland.

Even back then, I was one of the few that bucked the trend and didn't drink. In fact, I only had a drink when I was on England duty on about three occasions. That was it. I preferred having a drink when I could go under the radar a bit more – when I didn't have a Three Lions logo on my shirt, when I was at a gig maybe, certainly somewhere where I wasn't standing next to Gazza.

I was old-school in some respects, but not in terms of getting drunk when I was with England. It wasn't a moral thing or anything like that. And it wasn't that I didn't occasionally like to have a drink. I simply felt I had to be more professional just to be on an even footing with some of my England team-mates, who I considered to be a lot more talented than me. Sometimes I looked at them and felt like an impostor, probably because of my humble beginnings in non-league football. I never really rid myself of that feeling. Brian Clough, my manager at Nottingham Forest, had told me he wasn't sure I was good enough to play for England, and there were times when I looked at the other players in the squad and wondered if I agreed with him. Maybe they could get away with going out for a drink the night before training, but I knew I couldn't.

And that was before I put myself up against players from West Germany and Italy in important matches, when I knew I would have to be at my very best to stand a chance of competing with them. Some players would use training on a Monday, for instance, to blow away the cobwebs, but I knew that if I went out drinking, I'd lose my place in the team.

Our first game of the 1990 World Cup, against Ireland in Cagliari, was an affront to football. It was a disgrace. It was two teams kicking lumps out of each other. And that was it. We were in a group with Ireland, Holland and Egypt and because the Dutch were seen as the powerhouse of the group, both Ireland and England knew neither of us could afford to lose that first game. It was so bad that *La Gazzetta dello Sport*'s headline the next day was 'No Football Please, We're English'.

I felt nervous during the game, which we drew 1–1. Bobby Robson came over to me after the match and said, 'What's the matter with you, son?' He said I looked nervous. The truth is I *was* nervous. I hadn't really realised just how constraining it was going to be for me to play in a major tournament. 'I have given you twenty international caps for you not to be nervous today, son,' he said.

The result intensified the discussions about our formation. We played with four at the back against Ireland and even though 4-4-2 was our tried-and-trusted system, a lot of the players felt we were better-suited to playing with three central defenders.

The main catalyst for those discussions was Chris Waddle, who was playing for Marseille at the time and was a big fan of the 3-5-2 system.

Some of the media suggested that Bobby Robson had been overruled and forced into playing a different system, but it didn't feel like that to me. Not that I would have recognised player power back then. I was at Forest playing for Brian Clough. You didn't do player power with Brian Clough. The only way players showed their power in that dressing room was by nodding when he shouted abuse at you.

Robson was an intelligent coach. He was open-minded. He didn't resist the change of formation. I think he recognised it suited the playing resources we had. I saw Gary Lineker say recently that Sir Bobby had discussed the change in formation with him, Peter Shilton, Terry Butcher and Bryan Robson. That sounds about right.

From a selfish point of view, I wondered if it might affect my position, because Tony Dorigo was a more natural wing-back than me and I never felt I would automatically get picked, so just keeping my place in the team was my main consideration. You end up being selfish like that. You want to stay in the team. England being successful and me being on the bench would have been a poor tournament for me.

I didn't really know how to play wing-back, but I managed to keep my place anyway. I just charged up and down. In most of the matches at World Cup 90, me and the opposition wing-back simply cancelled each other out. I wasn't clever enough to know where I should be standing and how to adjust my position, so my contribution was not as substantial as I'd have liked.

At Forest, I was used to getting one-twos off Nigel Clough and running into spaces and surging forward. With England, when I gave it to John Barnes, I soon realised I wasn't going to be getting it back again. We didn't really complement each other like that. John Barnes was the bigger name and the better player by far, so I naturally deferred to him. He was a wonderful player and England icon, still an important part of the Liverpool side that had won the league title that season, which was the last time they lifted the trophy until Jürgen Klopp's team repeated the feat in 2020.

And apart from the fact that John Barnes had so much skill and wanted to use it, the system we were veering towards changed the way I played. When you are the wing-back, you are standing further up the pitch so you are not coming on to things. I would have lost my place to Dorigo if we had been playing that system for a year or more coming into the finals, but we hadn't, so I was retained.

We were wary of the Dutch when we faced them in the next match. They had an outstanding team. There was the famous triumvirate of Frank Rijkaard, Ruud Gullit and Marco van Basten and they were supplemented by other world-class players like Jan Wouters and Ronald Koeman.

We played much better than we had against Ireland and even though it was a 0–0 draw, the performance was hailed as a triumph for the sweeper system. Mark Wright played alongside Terry Butcher and Des Walker in the back three and Paul Parker and I were pushed up as wing-backs. Gazza was superb and he produced one Cruyff Turn in the second half that had everyone purring. The bigger the stage and the better the opposition, the more Gazza loved it.

That was the game we lost Bryan Robson. It felt like a big blow at the time when he limped off because he was a player of such stature, but David Platt replaced him that day and really stepped up. The longer the game went on, the more likely it seemed we were going to win it.

In fact, close to the end, I thought we had won it. We got a free kick on the right-hand side of their penalty area and I took it. I whipped it round the wall with my left foot and the Dutch goalkeeper, Hans van Breukelen, dived at full length to try to reach it but couldn't keep it out.

It was an indirect free kick but I celebrated the goal because I thought Van Breukelen, who had played for Forest until the season before I arrived there, had touched it on the way in. He told me later he had it covered but I think it beat him all ends up and he just couldn't get anywhere near it. Anyway, it didn't count.

That left us needing to get a result in the last group game, against Egypt, to be sure of going through to the second phase. It was another difficult, disjointed game and Egypt concentrated on getting men behind the ball and trying to frustrate us as we searched for the goal we needed.

We got it just before the hour. We won a free kick just inside the left-hand touchline and when Gazza curled it high into the box, Mark Wright produced a fantastic leap and got to it before the Egyptian goalkeeper and glanced it into the empty net. It wasn't pretty and we never really found any rhythm, but it didn't matter. It was a win and it got us through to a second-round match against Belgium.

*   *   *

We moved away from Sardinia for the first time and played the Belgians in Bologna. We got lucky, really. They were the better team and Enzo Scifo bossed the game from midfield. Scifo hit the post, Jan Ceulemans hit the post and even though John Barnes had a goal disallowed for offside, we were fortunate that we stayed in the game long enough for it to be heading towards a penalty shoot-out.

Then, in the last minute of extra time, Gazza, who was probably the only player on the pitch who still had the ambition and the confidence to believe that the game could be won before it went to spot kicks, broke out of defence and drove deep into the Belgium half.

He got to within about 40 yards of the Belgium goal when he was brought down. He floated a beautiful free kick into the path of David Platt. Platt watched it as it dropped over his shoulder and then swivelled to volley his shot past the Belgium goalkeeper. It was his first goal for England. It was a pretty decent way to score it. We were into the quarter-finals against Cameroon in Naples.

I watched that game again recently and I couldn't believe how bad we were. I very much include myself in that. Some of our defending was atrocious and most of our overall play wasn't much better. If you go to the well too often in the group stages and then go to extra time in your second-round match, it catches up with you later in the tournament. That was probably part of it.

And part of it was that we felt we would win the game comfortably. Cameroon had started the tournament by beating the holders, Argentina, but they had two players sent off in that match and by the time they reached the quarter-finals, they had four players suspended because of ill-discipline. We were told that we practically had a bye into the semi-finals.

But they were one of the great stories of that tournament. Their progress to that stage seemed to herald a new dawn for African football. It was obvious even then that African nations were emerging as a significant force in the game and that Cameroon side was at the forefront of that movement.

In my youth, I remember people laughing at Zaire in the 1974 World Cup, but people didn't laugh at African football any more. Cameroon were a fine team and we only underestimated them because they were so depleted. We underestimated them even after what they had done to Argentina.

I started to get an idea that that was probably rather a misguided and stupid notion just before the game. When we walked out of the changing rooms at the Stadio San Paolo in Naples we had to go along a corridor around the pitch and as both teams were striding along this together, the Cameroon players started singing. The captain began the chant and then the rest of the players joined in. They seemed incredibly confident and buoyed up. They looked like they were enjoying themselves already. Some of them were laughing. There was no sign of nerves at all. I remember thinking, 'What's going on here?'

Credit to them: they turned the game into a physical encounter and they took us right to the brink. We went ahead midway through the first half when I got away from my marker down the left wing and crossed to the back post, where David Platt was unmarked. He headed it down and past the Cameroon goalkeeper.

But at half-time they brought on their talisman, 38-year-old Roger Milla, and he changed the game. Gazza brought him down in the box and Cameroon scored from the spot, then a few minutes later Milla unlocked our defence with a clever run and pass and they took the lead.

If they had not been quite so naive in their defending, they would have beaten us, but Gary Lineker drew a foul seven minutes from the end and side-footed the penalty into the corner to draw us level. Midway through extra time, Lineker ran on to a beautiful through ball from Gazza and was brought down as he took the ball round the keeper. He blasted the ball down the middle this time to put us ahead.

I wouldn't say Lineker was a diver, but he had played in Spain and he was experienced. He was a clever player. He knew how to induce penalties. He knew where to place the ball to provoke a lunge. He was cute enough and wise enough and Cameroon fell for it. There is no doubt they were penalties and anyway, Cameroon weren't exactly angels. Lineker said afterwards their centre half was punching him off the ball on the halfway line.

Gary and I got on fine. We weren't the best of buddies. Slightly different individuals. I don't think football meant quite as much to him as it did to me. That is not a criticism. It is just an observation. Perhaps football meant too much to me and he had things more in perspective. Like I say, different individuals.

But what a striker he was. It is a measure of his quality and his temperament that he delivered on the biggest stage. Two World Cups and he delivered goals at both of them. Only seven players in history have scored more goals than him at the biggest tournament of them all and for two World Cups running, he delivered.

He wasn't a great trainer, but if you wanted someone to put the ball in the net, he was unbelievable. He hardly ever scored from outside the box but he had a gift for being in the right place in the penalty area. It's more than a gift, actually. It takes hard work and the willingness to make run after run after run. Five of the runs, the ball might not come your way, but the sixth time it will.

So his success was a reward for hard work and persistence as well as pure talent. I'd have him in the top five of the greatest English players of the last fifty years. I always felt he kept a little bit for himself, whereas the likes of Terry Butcher and Bryan Robson and Tony Adams gave everything to the team's cause, but that's a striker for you.

Anyway, we were through to face West Germany in Turin. After the mess of our performance against Cameroon, not many gave us a chance. But the rhythms of a tournament are hard to predict. A good performance can easily be followed by a bad one and vice versa. Everything, including the evolution of a side, seems to be heightened and quickened. It is as if you live through an entire season in the space of a few weeks.

We had played five matches before the game against West Germany and in the majority of them we had not been the better team. We had had some good fortune, the odd penalty and a flash of talent in the Belgium game. So it was hardly surprising that we went into the semi-final as underdogs. And we were tired. Lineker has said since that he felt we were all close to running on empty.

West Germany were a good side, too. They always seem to have the ability and the planning to peak at tournaments and 1990 was a case in point. Serie A was still the best league in the world then and they had that trio of players – Andreas Brehme, Lothar Matthäus and Jürgen Klinsmann – at Inter Milan who were the bedrock of their side. Matthäus, in particular, had started the tournament as if destined to be the best player in it.

But we went toe to toe with them that night in Turin. Everybody on our side came out with credit. Des Walker was arguably the best central defender in the world at that point and he had both Rudi Völler and his subsequent replacement Karl-Heinz Riedle in his pocket in that match. And they were both strikers of the highest quality.

Lineker had scored six goals at the 1986 World Cup and already had three more in Italy. Mark Wright was playing with some of the elegance of Bobby Moore in the new sweeper role. David Platt had emerged as a fine international player. Me? Look, I'm a left back. If we are going to win the game, it's going to be down to Lineker or Chris Waddle or John Barnes and not Stuart Pearce. My job is to stop the guy on the other team winning the game for them.

And we had Gazza, too. Gazza was probably our best player in that tournament. I saw an old BBC interview with Sir Bobby recently where he talked about him and what he was expecting from him in that semi-final against West Germany. It is easily forgotten that Gazza had only just squeezed into the squad at the last minute thanks to a bravura performance in a friendly against Czechoslovakia at Wembley at the end of April.

'Gascoigne had strayed in the match against Cameroon,' Sir Bobby said in the interview. 'I said to him, "Listen, if you do that against Germany, Matthäus will come striding through our midfield and stick two goals past Peter Shilton from 25 yards, because that's what he can do, so you can't chase the ball." "Boss," he said, "sit back and enjoy it, I know what I have to do."

'This is Gascoigne talking to me like this! So I looked at him and said, "I know you know what you have to do, but will you do it?" The fact he was going to play Matthäus thrilled him. He was going to adore that challenge and he was going to win it. And he did. He was better than Matthäus.'

We had been poor against Cameroon, but against West Germany we produced our best form of all our time in Italy. In fact, the way we played, the style we showed, the creativity we had with Gascoigne and the technical brilliance of a player like Waddle, it was a game that restored some faith in the England football team.

More than that, perhaps. It was the game that changed everything for English football. It was the game that allowed us to stop looking backwards and to create a new mood around the English game. What Gazza did that night, and how close we came and how well we played, helped to lay the foundations for the success of the Premier League and the dominant position our club football has now.

We just couldn't quite get the job done, though. We dominated the game in the first half, but they took the lead after an hour when I brought down Thomas Hässler on the edge of the box and Andreas Brehme's free kick deflected up off Paul Parker and looped over Peter Shilton.

There were ten minutes left when Parker lofted a hopeful ball forward and Lineker profited from confusion in the West German defence and drilled a left-foot shot across Bodo Illgner and into the bottom corner. You didn't often see me in goal celebrations, because I was usually too far back or trying to organise the defence ready for the restart, but you saw me in that one.

It was a great moment and I felt we were going to reach the final then. Waddle hit the post in extra time, but we couldn't quite force the winner and so it went to the penalty shoot-out.

2

NUMBER FOUR IS THE ONE THAT PUTS YOU OUT

T HE PENALTY SHOOT-OUT against West Germany at the 1990 World Cup was the biggest crime ever committed against English football. Not because of any injustice that was done to us. But because of the injustice we did to ourselves. It is hard to believe now, but when we came to the biggest moment in our football history since the 1966 World Cup final, our biggest moment for nearly a quarter of a century, we suddenly realised we hadn't prepared properly for it.

This is not a criticism of Sir Bobby Robson. It is more a comment on the times. It was virgin territory for us as an international team. It was the first penalty shoot-out England had been involved in and only the fourth for West Germany, but when I look back at it, I still find it astonishing that so little research had gone into choosing our penalty-takers. When Chris Waddle took our last kick in Turin, it was the first time he had ever taken a competitive penalty.

I suppose we had some sort of excuse in 1990 purely because it was so new. There was no backstory. Penalty shoot-outs were still a novelty in those days: this was only the twelfth in the history of the World Cup, European Championship and Copa América combined. We are conditioned now to the idea that the

Germans are automatons in shoot-outs and cannot be beaten, while we are flaky and weak, but none of that history existed thirty years ago. There was no inbuilt insecurity complex then.

So there was less of an excuse in 1996 when we went into that shoot-out with Spain in the quarter-finals. And yet nothing had really changed. There was still the same atmosphere of chaotic spontaneity about who wanted to take one. Even at the 1998 World Cup, when David Batty missed against Argentina, it was the first penalty he had ever taken. Why was that allowed to happen?

It was the same for a lot of nations, I think. When Jack Charlton died recently I watched some of the Ireland players reminiscing about their time under him when he managed their national team and one of the things they mentioned was their shoot-out against Romania at that World Cup in 1990. Jack struggled to find five people willing to take one, according to the Irish lads. They went through anyway.

Once we had beaten Egypt in the last of our group games at the 1990 World Cup, we did at least start to practise penalties. But there was no real organisation to it. It was very ad hoc. There was no defined taking order, not that we knew of anyway. There was no preparation for what would happen if we went to a shoot-out in one of our knock-out games. It was an afterthought.

So at the end of extra time in Turin, when a place in the World Cup final could have been just a few minutes away, the manager just gathered us together so that we could come up with five players. He asked who was up for it. We knew Gary Lineker would take one, because he was our designated penalty-taker, but after that it was up to individuals.

I was a penalty-taker for my club and I had absolutely no problem stepping forward. The way my mind worked, I would have had a problem staying quiet. Whatever club I played for, I would always back myself to be one of the best five penalty-takers and would be up for taking it, and that evening in Turin was no different.

England had only been awarded two penalties in the eight years leading up to the 1990 World Cup and I don't remember who was the designated penalty-taker in that time. I always assumed it was Lineker, and on the eve of going to Italy, Gary had asked Sir Bobby if the responsibility could be given to him. The manager knew the importance of scoring goals to any striker and so the decision was made.

Lineker took the first penalty in the shoot-out and sent Illgner the wrong way. Brehme took their first penalty and even though Shilton guessed the right way, diving low to his right, it was struck too well for him to get a hand on it. Peter Beardsley took our second penalty and hit it high to Illgner's left. Matthäus hit their second so hard that Shilton barely saw it. Platt scored our third. Riedle scored theirs.

And then it was my turn. I was the fourth penalty-taker. I don't know why I had been put in that position in the pecking order. I'm not sure anybody did. In later years, when I was the England Under-21 manager and I made it my business to be scientific about the art of penalty-taking, I found the data showed that penalty number one and penalty number four are statistically the most important penalties in the shoot-out.

Number four is the one that puts you out. Quite often, the fifth penalty is irrelevant. I didn't know that as I walked up to the spot in Turin. I did know that I would not have been able to live with myself if I had shrunk away and hidden and let someone else take all the heat and the pressure because I had lost my nerve even when I was the regular penalty-taker for Nottingham Forest.

That was never going to happen. I was always going to take one. I had seen the way the other players had taken theirs and I decided to slam mine down the middle. I considered slamming it down the middle the safer option. When you are being threatened, you go to a safe place. I think I went to a safe place.

I knew the goalkeeper was probably going to dive in one direction or the other. I thought if I put enough pace and power on the kick it would beat him. I thought I was giving myself two chances, because even if he guessed right and stayed where he was, there was still a decent possibility that he would be beaten by the power.

I ran up and smashed it. I hit it cleanly, but even though Illgner dived to his right, the ball cannoned off his right foot and away to safety. It was at a good height to be saved, I suppose, and that gave the goalkeeper a chance. 'Oh, and he's hit it too straight,' Martin Tyler said on the commentary, 'and West Germany find it's tilting their way.'

So maybe they thought I wasn't made of the right stuff any more. I was devastated. I sank to my haunches briefly. I knew instinctively in that second that our World Cup was almost certainly over. As I walked away from the penalty spot towards the halfway line, I thought, 'I'm going to be a very lucky man if someone digs me out of this one.' A couple of the players tried to console me. Lineker put his arm round me and ruffled my hair. I only know that because I've seen it on the replays. I couldn't really think of anything at the time. I was in a trance of misery.

By then, I didn't really think there was much chance of Shilton saving one. The German penalties had been too good up to that point. In the end, Shilton didn't get near any of the pens. His claim to fame is that he went the right way for all of them. Someone pointed out that if you only dive when they hit the back of the net, you've got a decent chance of going the right way.

That's a bit unkind, I know. I have seen Lineker say that he and Shilton discussed an approach to penalties during the tournament and that they had both noticed a lot of kicks were being struck down the middle. So Shilts had decided to stay on his feet as long as possible. As it happened, West Germany went for the corners every time.

He was always an arrogant so-and-so, Shilts. He was good at what he did, absolutely no doubt about that, but let me give you a small example of the kind of thing he got up to that would wind me up: when we got back to the dressing room after the Holland game, he came in and started calling Des Walker a cheat because he had allowed Marco van Basten to get a shot in.

Bear in mind that Des had had a brilliant game and bear in mind, too, that Van Basten will be remembered as one of the greatest strikers there has ever been and Des had kept him quiet. Remember that Des was a good friend of mine. I wasn't going to let that one go. When you call people cheats, that's quite strong. It implies a few things. I told Shilts in relatively forthright terms that it might be better if he kept his mouth shut on that occasion.

Shilts was like that with other players, too, to be fair to him. It wasn't just that he was picking on Des. I heard him berating

Bryan Robson once and telling him that he, Shilts, was the only world-class player in the England squad and talking about how many clean sheets he kept. Everyone respected him, but there wasn't an awful lot of warmth towards him.

Gazza was extremely good at poking fun at him. It became a standing joke that at every team meeting we had in 1990, whenever Sir Bobby asked if anybody had anything to say, Shilts would stand up and preface everything he said with 'Gaffer, I have got 118 caps, I know what I'm talking about . . .'

The next meeting, it would be 'Gaffer, I have got 119 caps, I know what I'm talking about . . .' and so on. Gazza latched on to this in the way that only he could and perfected a brilliant imitation of Shilts going through his routine. It had the rest of the squad in fits of laughter.

Occasionally, the squad would get its own back on Shilts. We had a race night at Is Molas one evening when we watched horse races that had been recorded for us on a video cassette. The idea was that we were watching them for the first time and we could bet on them as if they were live. Shilts loved his racing and he and Lineker were appointed the bookies.

Unbeknownst to them, though, Gazza had made sure the lads had got a sneak preview of the last race and so we all piled on the horse we knew was going to win. It came with a late run and the cheering in that room nearly blew the ceiling off. The look on Shilts's face was absolutely priceless. It took a little while, but we put him out of his misery in the end and told him the truth.

*   *   *

It wasn't that I blamed Shilts for the result of the penalty shoot-out. Not one bit. I only blamed one person and that was me. I looked at myself first. Especially with something as stark as this. I had missed from 12 yards. There was no way I could look around at someone else and think, 'If only they had done better.' I had missed a penalty that I felt had cost us a final place.

Hindsight is a wonderful thing and it is easy for us all to have our theories about what we might have done differently. Now that the shoot-out is regarded as something to prepare for thoroughly, maybe we would have tried something bolder to be ready for those kicks against the Germans.

I can see the logic in the idea that we could have brought Dave Beasant on just before the end of extra time to replace Shilton. Beasant had a good record at penalty saves. He was a specialist. He had made a crucial stop from a John Aldridge penalty in the 1988 FA Cup final when Wimbledon pulled off one of the great football shocks to beat Liverpool.

Martin O'Neill was going to do something similar in the 1996 First Division play-off final before his Leicester City side scored a last-minute winner, and Louis van Gaal used it to good effect in the 2014 World Cup when he replaced Jasper Cillessen with Tim Krul for the shoot-out in the match against Costa Rica and the Netherlands won 4–3 on penalties.

It wasn't an option in Turin, though. It would have been a hell of a call for Sir Bobby to replace Shilton, who had had a good tournament. But it would have been impossible to bring Beasant on anyway, because he wasn't even among the substitutes. You were only allowed five substitutes in those days and Chris Woods was the replacement goalkeeper.

If Beasant was on the bench, he was sitting on it in a suit and tie.

After my penalty was saved, Olaf Thon was next up for West Germany. He did a little shimmy in his run-up and hit his kick low and hard to Shilton's left. Shilts went the right way again but didn't get anywhere near it. That meant our next penalty-taker, Chris Waddle, needed to score for us to stay in the competition.

I think Gazza would have taken that fifth penalty, but he wasn't in any fit state to do so. He had been booked in extra time, the booking that famously prompted Lineker to look over to the bench and warn them that poor Gazza was distraught. The booking meant he would miss the final if we got there, and his bewilderment was written all over his face.

It was no consolation for me at the time, but even if we had won that penalty shoot-out, I'm not sure that we would have gone on to win the final. Argentina, the other finalists, were not as good as West Germany, but we would have been much diminished without Gazza.

Waddle took the kick. He went for power and height. If it had gone in, it might have burst the net, but it didn't go in. He hit it too high and it flew over the bar and away into eternity. I don't blame him, either. I knew our tournament was over when I missed. What Chris did was irrelevant. They would have scored the fifth penalty if they had needed to. We weren't well enough prepared. It's as simple as that.

There is a pattern when you look at the people who have missed penalties that have put us out of tournaments: Chris

Waddle had never taken a competitive penalty, neither had David Batty before he stepped up against Argentina at the 1998 World Cup. Gareth Southgate was not a regular penalty-taker when he took his at Euro 96. It's not rocket science. Lack of preparation has a habit of finding you out.

It was a bad way to go out of the tournament. We felt as though the performance against West Germany deserved more. We had been growing as a team and as individuals. It is inevitable that we talk about Gazza's antics off the pitch, because he was larger than life, but on the pitch he was developing into one of the best players in the world. He went to that tournament and he seized it. He left his mark on it and he left his mark on the English game, too.

Gazza was as responsible as anyone for the transformation in domestic football that we can still see today in the prosperity of the Premier League. He was the face of it. When we arrived in Italy for that World Cup, we were still regarded as the Sick Man of Europe in terms of the behaviour of our fans. Our football was defined by disasters like Heysel and Hillsborough. It was about sorrow and grief. Gazza's brilliance and his exuberance helped to change all that. Some people laugh at him, but the force of his personality carried everyone along with him. His tears at the end of the match against West Germany became a symbol, ironically, of the way England had fallen in love with football again.

The joy of what happened at the 1990 World Cup brought a new dawn for the English game. English football had spent too long treating supporters like dirt and penning them into cages like animals, and there were occasions when the fans let themselves down, too. But now everything began to change. The Taylor Report introduced a requirement for all-seater stadiums at top-flight English grounds and English football began to move towards an American model, where supporters were treated as customers and facilities at stadiums were like something you might find at a cinema rather than in a cattle shed.

After 1990, families started coming back to the game. There was a cost, in that a lot of traditional fans were priced out of the new Premier League, but kids could go to games without the fear of being caught up in hooligan violence. Roy Keane talked about the 'prawn sandwich brigade' of corporate fans who started coming to English football in the 1990s, and he was right about that, but the game found more of a balance in terms of allowing people to enjoy going to stadiums in safety and comfort again.

Gazza went to play in Serie A a couple of years after the tournament. In those days it was a mark of real class if an English player went to play abroad and succeeded. But 1990 began to change that as well. Soon, it wasn't Serie A that we were looking to as the gold standard for European football any more.

What Gazza and Sir Bobby's England team in 1990 helped to set in motion was a transformation of the way English football was regarded. We were not seen as pariahs any more. And as investment flooded into our game and our clubs began to grow more wealthy and the television deals grew in profitability, the best players wanted to come to the Premier League, not Serie A.

Gazza left Spurs for Lazio in 1992, but because of him, the world's best players started heading in the opposite direction later in the decade. Dennis Bergkamp, Patrick Vieira and Thierry Henry came to Arsenal; Gullit and Gianfranco Zola came to

Chelsea; Eric Cantona and Juan Sebastián Verón came to Manchester United and so on and so on.

The truth is that 1990 was the start of the gold rush for the English game and for the Premier League, even though it wasn't actually born yet. That World Cup laid the foundations for everything that was to come and the prosperity that is still improving the English game year after year.

By the time I came off the pitch in Turin, I was in tears, too. I was lucky I had three other players from Forest who knew me well enough to help me get through it. These were the people who knew me inside out: Des Walker, Steve Hodge and Neil Webb. Having them around me was massive. Throw Terry Butcher into the mix on that, too.

Some of the players went over to the England fans but, to be honest with you, I just wanted to get off the pitch. I was done. I was wrung out. Neil Webb threw me a towel and I put it over my head so I could hide my face. I felt like a criminal. No one else had made me feel like that, but I couldn't change it. I prided myself on my strength of character and yet it was me who had let the rest of the lads down. I got in the dressing room and when the other boys started filing in, there were a lot of tears. It was very, very sombre.

A couple of German players came in. They weren't trying to rub it in. They weren't like that. One of them – Thomas Berthold – had asked to swap shirts with me. Berthold was the player who had been fouled by Gazza when Gazza got the yellow card that upset him so much. Some of our lads felt he had rolled around rather too enthusiastically.

A couple of our boys told them to get lost. Steve Hodge was one of the lads who got upset, but I told him I had asked Berthold to come in. I never liked to swap my England shirt on the pitch. I didn't like the idea of coming off with a foreign shirt on my back. I used to do it in the tunnel.

While I was sitting there, trying to collect myself, I felt a tap on the shoulder from Doc Crane, the England team doctor. He said Shilts and I had been selected as the players who had to do the drugs test. It was the last thing I wanted, to be taken away from the rest of the lads at a moment like that, to be taken away from the dressing room, which was as close to a sanctuary as you could get. You want the togetherness of the people who have had the same experience as you. That was taken away from me straight away.

It is an emotionally important time for a squad when you have just gone out of a tournament. And the worst time to lose is in a semi-final. If you lose in a final, there are no more games and everyone goes home. After a semi-final, you have to hang around for the third-place play-off, which is horrible. It is like being consigned to a few days of torture, parading your grief in public when all you want to do is disappear.

I walked down a couple of corridors and was led into a small, featureless room. I don't think Shilts even sat down. Goalkeepers don't get as dehydrated as outfield players, so he walked in, provided his urine sample and walked straight out again. It wasn't so simple for me.

I must have been there for an hour. I was drinking pint after pint of water and I still couldn't pee. It was the same for the two German players who had been picked out. I didn't want to look at anyone or speak to anyone. I just sat there with my head down. I didn't say a word.

What happened in that room left a big impression on me, though. Because the two West Germany players didn't say a word either. They must have felt like singing and dancing. They had just made it through to the World Cup final, but they had so much respect for their opponent – me – and so much dignity, that they were silent, too.

As I sat there, I wondered whether, if the roles were reversed, two English players would have been as restrained as they were if England had won that semi-final. I wondered if we would have been as dignified as that. I wondered if we would have had that much respect for a German opponent. I hope so, but I'm not sure.

They taught me a valuable lesson in how to be humble with victory that day. I sat there with my head bowed. They sat there and did not say a word to each other for the best part of an hour. Not a word. If someone had come into that room, they would not have known who had won and who had lost. I don't even know who they were. I didn't look up enough to know who they were.

After about an hour, they both finally managed to give their samples and left. In an attempt to take my mind off giving my sample, I walked the perimeter of the stadium with Doc Crane – the rest of the team had got showered and changed and were on the bus – and it felt so strange being there in the quiet, with only the cleaners and a few security guards rattling around in the stands.

I had left a full stadium, with the emotion of everything going on and dreams newly shattered, and now there was barely a soul there. The cleaners were picking up litter and putting it into their plastic bags. All I could hear was the sound of seats being lifted into the upright position.

*　　*　　*

In the end, I managed to give a sample and was able to go and join the others on the bus. I found a seat on my own and big Butch came and sat next to me on the journey back to the hotel. It was a nice gesture and I knew why he was doing it, but I would rather have been on my own. I didn't want to talk to anyone. I could barely speak anyway.

I cried for the whole journey. The only time I've ever really cried was then and after Euro 96. I am very hardened to football and what it offers, but in 1990 I felt I had let everyone down, including my family. My ex-wife, Liz, and my mum and dad had come out to Italy and I felt like I had let them down. I felt like I had let everybody down.

We got back to the hotel. Some of the players went for something to eat in the restaurant. I went straight to bed. We shared rooms in those days and I was with Des Walker. He could talk the hind legs off a donkey. He'd talk and talk and talk. I'd turn the lights out at half ten and he'd still be talking. He'd often talk himself to sleep. On this occasion, we didn't say a word to each other. He knew.

I had drunk so much bloody water at the stadium that I kept getting up to go to the toilet. I must have done that five times. In the end, I got a tin wastepaper basket and put it next to the bed and every time I needed to go, I rolled over and peed out of the side of the bed. It was like a machine gun. I'd filled it up by the morning.

I wanted to go home but we had to play the third-place play-off game and we travelled from Turin down to Bari, in the south of the country. Bobby said he was going to leave me out. It was the last thing in the world I wanted. My only thought was that people would think I wasn't mentally strong enough to handle it and that I'd been destroyed by what happened in the shoot-out.

He left Chris Waddle out, too, and he was going to omit Shilts, but Shilts talked him out of it. Shilts said it would put him on 125 caps and it was the last England game of his career. Bobby relented and Shilts played. I sat there and watched. I was miserable, but I understood why Bobby had done it: Tony Dorigo had not kicked a ball all tournament and deserved more. I liked Tony very much and I knew it was the fair thing to do.

We lost to Italy in Bari. Shilts made a mistake twenty minutes from the end when he lost concentration and allowed Roberto Baggio to steal the ball off him and then rifle a shot into the roof of the net. Platty equalised with a header from a lovely cross by Dorigo, but in the last few minutes, Italy got a penalty. One last chance for Shilts to save a spot kick, but Toto Schillaci sent him the wrong way to win the game. At least Schillaci came away from the game with the consolation of having won the tournament's Golden Boot. We left with nothing.

We finally flew home the day after the game. I just wanted to get in my car and head back to Nottingham, but when we landed at Luton there were 300,000 people waiting to welcome us. It was the most surreal thing I have ever seen. I hadn't realised quite how much what we had done had captured the imagination of the public.

We got on an open-top bus and what should have been a fifteen-minute journey from the airport to the Hilton Hotel at Junction 11 took us five or six hours. Most of the players headed up to the top deck, but at that stage Chris Waddle and I thought we were more likely to get lynched than cheered so we took our seats downstairs and let the rest of the lads lap up the applause.

We soon sensed how celebratory the mood was and we both went up the stairs to join the other lads and sat up there for the duration. It wasn't just the reception that day that touched me: I got a lot of letters from not just Forest fans but Derby fans and all sorts that were very supportive.

It was testimony, I think, to how much the nation had been gripped by what we had done. After so many years of bad news and grieving around English football, at club and international level, this felt like a rare burst of good news. It changed the mood.

My persona changed from that moment, too. From being a club player playing a bit of international football, I felt like I was now an established international, with more stature at my club.

Not that it helped me when I asked Brian Clough if I could have a fortnight off when we got back. I arrived home on 8 July and he said he was expecting me in training on 9 July. Forest had pre-season games to fulfil and he didn't want me trying to play the big-time Charlie just because I'd been at a World Cup. He wanted to make sure I kept my feet on the floor. He needn't have worried about that. There's nothing like missing the most important penalty in your nation's history to make certain you don't misplace your humility.

In many ways, I wanted to get straight back into it anyway. I wanted to put Turin behind me as fast as I could. I remember people saying the same thing about David Beckham after he was turned into a scapegoat when England were knocked out of the 1998 World Cup. Sir Alex Ferguson told him to get back to Manchester United as quickly as he could and they would look after him.

And they did look after him. He might have been vilified elsewhere, but United threw a protective shield around him, and it was the same for me when I got back to Forest. I felt bolstered and supported and I was burning to show everyone I was strong enough to deal with what had happened in Turin. And the 1990–91 season was my best season by a million miles.

I scored sixteen goals in domestic competitions and felt I had something to prove on a daily basis. Anybody who thought I was going to go under, I showed them. If you think I'm going to shy away from any sort of challenge just because I've missed a penalty, you are sadly mistaken. I scored those goals, Forest got to the FA Cup final and I was named one of the PFA's six best players of the year.

Everywhere I went, I had opposition fans yelling 'Stuart Pearce is a German' at me, but it really didn't bother me. It motivated me, if anything. I'm the kind of person who thrives off that kind of stuff. In fact, if I'd scored that penalty in Turin, I'm not sure I would have come out and rolled my sleeves up in quite the same way. I was ready for a fight.

3

TERRY VENABLES AND AN OLD WARHORSE

THERE WERE TIMES in the next six years when I thought I would not survive in the England team long enough to make the 1996 tournament. I was desperate to play in it, of course. I am a patriot and playing for my country was the best thing that ever happened to me in my career, so the idea of a home European Championship was the kind of thing that made the hairs on the back of my neck stand up.

But six years is a long time in international football and there were some highs and lows along the way. Graham Taylor took over as England manager after Sir Bobby Robson left for PSV and I became one of his key players. He and I got on well and he trusted me. His reign has been heavily criticised and he made some mistakes, but he was not dealt the best hand, either.

I started every game at Euro 92 in Sweden, but that was a miserable tournament for us. We had an ordinary side compared to the team of two years earlier and we struggled. We drew our first two games without scoring and then lost to Sweden in our third. That was the game when Taylor substituted Lineker in what was to be his last England match. We were on the way home almost before we arrived.

Lineker was the captain for that tournament and after he

retired from the international game, Taylor came round to my house and asked if I would like to replace him as skipper. It was a great honour, obviously, but my captaincy didn't exactly coincide with a glorious part of England's football history. Those were the years of 'Do I not like that'. We failed to qualify for the 1994 World Cup in the USA.

I felt sorry for Graham. Like Sir Bobby Robson, he was a good man. And like Sir Bobby, he was ridiculed by the press. After we lost that Sweden game in 1992, *The Sun*'s headline was 'Swedes 2, Turnips 1' and Graham's head was made to look like a turnip. It was a cruel way to treat someone and he struggled to shake it off.

He never got any luck, either. It probably wasn't a very good idea to allow a camera crew to shadow him during the doomed qualification campaign for the 1994 World Cup, and the resulting documentary, *An Impossible Job*, didn't paint him in a particularly good light. He was a man who deserved better.

Terry Venables took over from Graham at the start of 1994 and he phoned me soon afterwards. Graeme Le Saux had joined Kenny Dalglish's Blackburn Rovers team in 1993 and had matured into a superb left back and Terry wanted to tell me that I would not be first choice for his England team. That would be Graeme. I understood the subtext, too. He wanted me to retire.

I really appreciated his honesty. I work better like that. He said, 'You're not my number one. What do you want to do about it?' I have been a manager and I know that when you make phone calls like that, you want the outcome to be 'Thank you very much, I'll go quietly.' It solves a problem. I was almost 32 and me falling on my sword would get rid of an old warhorse who had been a decent servant for the country.

Terry was smart. He was thinking he didn't want to be the one to put my lights out. He would rather I did it myself. It's a respectful thing to do in a way. I can understand why he did it. He thought my legs were going a little bit. Things like that are in the mix. Sometimes, you can lead the player to the door and let him walk through it. They come out with a touch more credit, even if it's to your detriment at times. That's the nature of the game.

I respected what Terry said, but I wasn't ready to walk away from England. I was prepared to stand my ground and fight for my place. But from that moment on I knew that at a basic level Terry didn't fancy me as a player. So it was always in my mind that if someone better came along, he would drop me like a stone.

That conversation motivated me for the rest of my time with England under Terry. It stayed with me. It was always there, gnawing at me. It wasn't a bad thing. It just kept me on my toes. I knew that I had to be giving it absolutely everything to have a chance of staying in his plans, because his natural inclination was to go with somebody else.

One area where I was lucky was that Terry was not averse to playing three central defenders and playing full backs as central defenders when he needed to or wanted to. I had played all my school football as a central defender, so it was not an unusual transition for me in some ways, and that gave me a new lease of life.

At least I knew where I stood with Terry. He liked flair players. He liked Nick Barmby and Gazza and Teddy Sheringham, clever players, good technical players, tactically aware players. I was a bit functional in comparison and I knew I had a battle on my hands if I wanted to stay in the squad.

There were other reasons why Euro 96 might never have happened for me. Some time in 1995, I received an offer to go and play for Kobe in Japan. I really liked the idea. I was fascinated by Japanese culture and by then I had developed a real interest in travel and experiencing other ways of life. I liked the idea of exposing myself to a new environment.

Maybe that's another thing that might surprise people about me. The fact that I love playing for England doesn't disqualify me from being fascinated by other cultures and from wanting to immerse myself in them. Here's something else: I enjoy reading Oscar Wilde. And if I could choose a group of people to bring along to a dinner party, the Marx Brothers would be on my guest list. This might not surprise people quite so much, but so would Adrian Edmondson, who played the punk in *The Young Ones*. I loved that show and I love punk and I love that character. Ade formed a punk band called The Bad Shepherds and I've been to see them play. He's a top man.

I talked to Kobe and they offered me a package, but it soon became apparent that the only way it would work financially was if Nottingham Forest were to release me on a free transfer, and Frank Clark, the manager at the time, was unwilling to do that. If I had gone, it almost certainly would have cost me my place in the England team. The penalty against Spain, my act of redemption in the eyes of the nation, would never have happened.

But at the time I wasn't sure I would even make it to Euro 96 with England. I kept going back to that conversation with Terry. And I didn't want to miss out on an interesting move because of something that might never happen. I'm glad now that I didn't move, obviously, because Euro 96 was the most rewarding experience of my career, but you never know what life is going to throw at you.

I suppose the critical moment in the build-up to the tournament, from the point of view of my prospects of featuring in it, came when I benefited from a horrible stroke of bad luck that afflicted Graeme Le Saux.

I had started the last World Cup qualifier against San Marino in November 1993 – and gave away a goal with an under-hit back pass in the first ten seconds – but after Terry Venables took over, I was moved aside. Graeme started at left back in eleven of the next twelve games and played extremely well. He scored a brilliant goal against Brazil in the summer of 1995 and it had got to the point where I knew it was going to be a struggle to get back in the England side. He had made the position his own.

Unusually for two players vying for the same position, Graeme and I got on really well together. We shared a musical interest – I liked punk, he was into indie music – so we used to talk music a lot and from the moment he came into the squad, we hit it off.

Our age difference was helpful as well, because I had a multitude of caps already and even though he was a rival for the position, I saw him as an apprentice who was the next one through the door. I knew I didn't have much more time on the clock. If we had been a similar age, I'm not sure our relationship would have been as good. But Graeme is a nice fella.

He suffered a lot at the hands of old-school players at Chelsea when he started out, and some people might be tempted to lump me in with that mentality of being suspicious of someone with his interests. People misjudge me a little bit like that. The music united us, but I liked the theatre as well. When I was playing at Newcastle, I would go in the afternoons on my own to watch *West Side Story* or Gilbert and Sullivan – that type of thing. So Graeme and I would share that interest as well. People thought I was two-dimensional. Their impression of me was that I kicked everything that moved, whether it be on the football pitch or off it, but there was a bit more to me than that.

I almost saw myself as a mentor to Graeme. I was never vindictive to him and I wanted to put him out of the team because of the way I was performing, not because he fell on his face doing something. I wanted him to play well, but I wanted me to play better.

Graeme was Terry's type of player. He was quick, he was mobile, he hared up and down the wing. He was also playing in a fine team at Blackburn. His career was very much on an upward trajectory.

I wasn't doing particularly well at keeping him out of the team, but then in September 1995 Graeme got a nasty ankle injury in a Premier League match against Coventry City. He managed to get over that and played his way back into the Blackburn team, only to be carried off during a 1–0 victory over Middlesbrough at Ewood Park in mid-December.

It was obvious from the footage of the incident, which happened when Graeme tackled Juninho and then landed awkwardly, that he had sustained serious damage. It soon emerged he had a broken tibia, a dislocated ankle and a ruptured tendon in his right leg. He was out of Euro 96.

I didn't want Graeme to suffer that. I didn't want to get back into the side that way. But I didn't talk to him after his injury. I didn't phone him or anything like that. Looking back over my career, I wish I had done that a bit more. I wish I had looked beyond myself more.

I think John Terry started doing that kind of thing when he was Chelsea captain, making phone calls to players out on loan, helping people settle, offering support when it was needed. It wasn't my way but maybe it should have been. Anyway, suddenly I was back in. Terry Venables needed me again.

Terry and Glenn Hoddle were the two best coaches I have worked with in terms of their tactics. I know this is irrelevant to his ability, but I was always impressed by the way Terry tied his boots like they did on the continent. Terry used to tie his laces up his leg. I think the Spanish players must have done that and he caught on to it while he was in charge of Barcelona.

I haven't mentioned Brian Clough in that top two for the simple reason he never spent much time with us on the training pitch. Brian's coaching came at half-time. There would be the odd piece of advice here and there, though. When I first came into the game, I had a habit of going to ground and making a lot of slide tackles. Brian got his hands on me and said, 'If you keep sliding on your arse, I will send you back to non-league.'

That is great coaching but it is not in the purest manner. He put the onus on you as a player or as a team. You didn't do set plays. You had to work it out for yourself. Stand next to someone you can beat in the air and mark them and win the ball. I never sat with Brian and talked tactics. There was no video analysis.

Terry was different. He was spot on as a coach. Chopping and changing between a three and a four at the back were indicators of a coach who was switched on tactically. His assistant Don Howe took the back four a lot. He was pretty hands on. He loved defensive work. Terry would work across the board. His time abroad had served him well. You always had that impression. He was streetwise. He knew how to work the press and the players.

The press was obsessed with the Christmas Tree formation – 4-3-2-1 – that Terry liked, but we didn't actually play it that often. We started Euro 96 playing 4-4-2 against Switzerland and adapted it to 3-5-2 against Scotland, before reverting to 4-4-2 for the final group game against the Dutch. We were back to a 3-5-2 against the Germans in the semi-final, with me playing on the left-hand side of the back three. Terry was at ease with different systems.

He was a clever man-manager, too. He knew how to give Gazza enough rope and then pull him back in again. He knew how to work all of us. He was far cuter than any of us players. He would give Gazza a ticking-off in front of all the squad and then, as he turned away, just wink at a couple of the players to show he didn't really care if Gazza was messing around a bit.

Tony Adams told me once that when Terry dropped David Platt when Platty was captain, Tony asked Terry if Platty would be upset by that. Tony felt a bit concerned. He was worried about taking Platty's place as skipper, which was the way it turned out throughout the tournament. Terry wasn't bothered. He said he'd deal with him later. He knew the tricks. He had been a manager a long time.

He was an amiable guy, but he could be ruthless, too. He was a football intellectual, but his brain gave him the touch of arrogance he needed to be ruthless. And I liked the enthusiasm he had for the game. He loved talking about football. He was one of those guys who would sit down at dinner and move salt and pepper pots around on the table when he was talking about tactics.

He was interested in people, too. He was close to a few of the press boys, I think. And they liked him because sometimes he socialised with them and he enjoyed their company. He liked hearing about their business, too. He was fascinated by it. He also had some enemies in the press, people who were critical of his business dealings and said he wasn't the right kind of person to be England manager, but he had plenty of friends, as well.

He certainly didn't get a free ride. We weren't playing great football as we got closer to Euro 96 and it is easy to forget now, in these days when we almost fill Wembley even for friendlies, but back then the crowds for England matches weren't great. In the season leading up to the Euros, we played Colombia, Switzerland, Portugal, Bulgaria, Croatia and Hungary at Wembley and the biggest crowd of all of them was 34,184 against Hungary, our final home game before the tournament started. Barely 20,000 turned up for the game against Colombia.

And how about this for a statistic: the Division Three play-off finals of 1994, 1995 and 1996 all attracted higher attendances than England games at Wembley around the same time, against Greece, Japan and Hungary respectively.

Euro 96 is remembered as something that united the nation, but there were few signs we were about to capture the public imagination in the build-up to it. Other managers might have lost their nerve. Maybe they would have changed the way they were playing or the personnel. Terry didn't.

That was another thing I admired about Terry: he was a strong manager. He didn't bend to the public will or to media pressure. That was evident in the way he stuck by Alan Shearer. When the tournament started, Shearer hadn't scored for England since September 1994. That was twelve games, and there was a lot of pressure for him to start Les Ferdinand or Robbie Fowler instead.

But Terry didn't waver. He stuck with Alan. In fact, he told him quite a long way out from the tournament that as long as he was fit, he would be in his starting line-up for the first game. It was a huge vote of confidence. Alan was a strong personality anyway, but when someone has that kind of faith in you, it is a great boost.

Alan inspired confidence in his team-mates, too. I felt that with him leading the line, we had a good chance of winning the tournament. He was that good. He was hard-nosed. He had a strong personality. Look at the England starting XI for the Euros and there was a lot of leadership quality in those ranks. Alan fell into that category.

The record books show that he didn't play for the most fashionable clubs, so the number of goals he scored is even more impressive, given that he may not have had the best supply lines. You always had the feeling with him that he was not going to go under through any lack of courage. He was never going to hide.

He was never going to shrink. He wasn't the kind of player who would fade away.

Going into a major tournament after a run like that, some strikers might have lost their confidence or their self-belief. Not Alan. He had faith in his own ability and because of that, I always felt it would turn for him. Terry obviously did, too. You go into a major tournament, though, and the pressure gets cranked up even more. Tournaments are not normally places where you can turn a bad goalscoring run into a good one. But he did.

I wasn't worried about the run he was on, but I was aware of it. When you think about who's going to win you the tournament, you are relying on Alan to get you the goals, to keep you in the game if it's not going your way and to close it out if you're on top. It was a strong squad in terms of strikers, but Alan was always going to be the man leading the line.

He probably wasn't the dominant personality in the squad, though. That was Tony Adams. I didn't know it, but Tony was going through a lot of problems at the time. It is well documented now that he had a drinking problem and a lot of demons, but it is a tribute to him that he never let any of that affect his game. He was one of the people I enjoyed spending time with off the pitch and I didn't know he had an issue.

It was a different time then. Sure, I knew there was a drinking culture at Arsenal. I knew there was a group of them that enjoyed going out on benders. But there was a drinking culture at most clubs back then. It was seen as normal, part of the game, particularly at club level. It was what a lot of people did to bond and build team spirit.

Tony wasn't England captain going into the tournament. David Platt had been given that honour, but Platty missed the first game against Switzerland and was injured for the second game against Scotland. When we got on a bit of a roll, Venables told him he was sticking with Tony as the skipper. We all felt for Platty, but it was hard to argue against Tony as captain.

Tony was a supreme organiser. In my first England game, in 1987, Tony played next to me in defence. I was older than him but he was the one marshalling people. He must have been born that way. I'm a big fan of his. The thing I admired most about him was that even when things weren't going well for him as an individual, he would help somebody else, which was the sign of a fantastic leader and a fantastic captain.

Tony had that about him. He had organisation, personality, a bit of everything. To have him alongside you was great. The mark of a good leader is somebody who cares about the others as much as himself. That was Tony. He was team-motivated above every-thing else.

My defining memory of him was that before every game at Euro 96, fifteen minutes before kick-off, he was having injec-tions into his knee so he could get through the game. Every game. I just kept praying he would make it to the end of the tournament. He was so important to us. You would struggle to name a better leader than Tony Adams in English football.

In that regard, he was head and shoulders above everyone else on the pitch. And there was a strong field. I was used to captain-ing. Gareth Southgate was a leader. There was Alan and Paul Ince. Plenty of leadership there. It is not often now you can look around a side and see captains all over the pitch, but that team had them everywhere.

We thought of Tony as our leader, though. And this was his chance. Bobby Robson had sprung a surprise by leaving him out of the squad for the 1990 World Cup, he was injured for the 1992 European Championship and we missed out on qualification for the World Cup in the USA in 1994, so this was his opportunity to shine on the big stage and he took it.

Disappointingly for someone who broke into the England squad at a young age and was made Arsenal captain when he was 21, he had not had a defining tournament experience and left his mark on it, so it was definitely his time. He made the most of it, just as he made the most of the rest of his career. He played on until 2002, notching up more than 600 appearances for Arsenal – a one-club man and a legend.

I would probably throw Incey into the mix as well in terms of characters who drove us on. He was playing at Inter Milan at the time and I think it helped his confidence that he was playing in Serie A and that he was loved by the crowd at the San Siro.

If you get the opportunity to go to Italy and you thrive out there, chances are your confidence will rise. He was not shy at coming forward anyway, but I looked at him and thought he had improved a few notches as a player even from the time when he was at Manchester United, and he was a top-class player then.

He and I got on fine. We weren't great friends off the pitch or anything like that, but I had total respect for him as a player. I flared up at him during a game between Forest and Manchester United in 1994 but I apologised to him the day afterwards. I liked the fire that was in him. He was a superb midfielder. He was someone you wanted on your side.

Teddy Sheringham was a strong personality, too; Gazza led from the front in terms of the way he was not awed by any opponent and his confidence transmitted itself to the rest of the team; Gareth's leadership skills have become more and more evident with every month he has been in charge of the current England side; and David Seaman was the best goalkeeper in the world at that time.

Seaman inspired confidence in a different way from Shilton. I always got the impression Shilton was after a clean sheet for Peter Shilton. Which is fine. He was very vocal and he was such a good goalkeeper that it helped us as a group of defenders. Dave was a different animal, totally. He had a quiet confidence. He was in sensational form at that time as well. If you are going to win a tournament or come close, you have to have a top-quality goalkeeper in great form – and that's exactly what we had.

If you were facing up the pitch, you wouldn't hear him for ninety minutes, and maybe in the early days of playing together, I took him for granted occasionally. There was one time at Wembley when he threw the ball out and it was just behind me, so I wasn't able to take it in my stride. I turned round and gave him some verbal abuse.

He certainly came out of his shell then. He told me not to call him the particular word I'd used. We smiled at each other and I told him I wanted the ball thrown in front of me so I could get on the front foot. 'Don't throw it behind me, that's my point,' I said. He said, 'I take your point, but be careful how you word it.'

We eyeballed each other for a moment. It was quite a nice moment. I said, 'All right, big man,' and then a little smile started playing on his face. You couldn't walk over him. He'd draw a line in the sand, but he'd do it in a quiet way.

When we were defending set pieces, you would hear Tony Adams more than Dave. But you knew the presence was there and that was the important thing. A lot of goalies shout their mouth off and there's no substance behind it. Dave wasn't one of those. Physically he filled the goal as well, which helped. He was a massive part of why we got as far as we did.

We needed our goalkeeper to be at his best in the same way that we needed our centre forward to be scoring goals. And Terry was strong enough to stick with Alan Shearer, because Terry was a confident man himself. He didn't worry about trying to please the media. I liked that about him. He was an independent thinker. He always had been since he was a player.

I remember reading that when some of his team-mates at Chelsea went to the snooker hall after training, Terry would go home to do some writing or reading. He was criticised by some people for having outside interests and I found that odd. Usually, footballers are criticised for being boring and insular and not interested in the world around them. Terry was the complete opposite of that.

His outside interests never affected his focus as far as I was concerned, but they did have an impact on his time in charge of England. He had a lot of business issues and he appeared to have made quite a lot of enemies in high places. I have read that was one of the reasons the FA wanted him to be known as the England coach rather than the England manager.

Four months after he took over from Graham Taylor, he lost a high-court battle with Sir Alan Sugar. Soon afterwards, police dropped an inquiry into allegations Venables had paid Brian

Clough a 'bung' to arrange the transfer of Teddy Sheringham to Spurs. The football world was agog at all of this.

In January 1996, Venables announced he would be standing down as England coach after Euro 96 because of a whole range of court cases due to be heard later in the year, which he felt would compromise England's attempts to qualify for the 1998 World Cup.

He and the FA seemed to be playing a game of brinksmanship. Terry blamed the court cases in public, but in private he was said to be upset that the FA would not offer to extend his contract for more than a year after the Euros. Before the 1990 World Cup, it had become known that Bobby Robson would be leaving after the tournament. Now the same was happening with Terry.

Again, a lot was made of it in the press. And there were plenty of unfavourable headlines. But it really didn't make any difference to us as players. It is not exactly unusual for a manager to leave after a major tournament. It is a natural break point in the cycle of an international side and it is not the sort of thing that players pay much attention to. I felt it was a shame that he was being lost to the FA, but it was above my pay grade. I got on with my job.

Terry understood how to handle players. Even if you were not one of his favourites and you knew you were not one of his favourites, he was too smart to make you feel like you were on the outside. Harry Redknapp was brilliant at that, as well. Good managers make players think they are loved, even if some are loved more than others.

Venables could read people. Like Sir Bobby Robson, he knew how to get the best out of them. Look at the performances he coaxed out of Darren Anderton and Steve McManaman, say, at Euro 96. I know they were both very talented players and Macca won the Champions League with Real Madrid, but they both played some of their best football during the tournament.

4

REFUELLING HABITS

A FORTNIGHT BEFORE WE were due to play our first match at Euro 96, we flew to the Far East to play a match against China and then an unofficial game in Hong Kong against a local XI. The general plan was to go so far away that our fans couldn't cause any problems at the match on the eve of the tournament and throw everything into doubt again.

The last thing we wanted was for Uefa to be threatening to throw us out of our own tournament. Colin Moynihan might have been up for that kind of thing six years earlier, but it really wouldn't have been a very good look this time around. Anyway, the part about playing thousands of miles away to stop the fans causing problems worked fine. It was just the players' behaviour that the FA hadn't bargained for.

We met up on a Saturday night at Burnham Beeches, the Buckinghamshire hotel that was our regular base and where we would be staying for the tournament. And then we waited for Paul Gascoigne. Gazza had been in the Rangers side that had beaten Hearts in the Scottish Cup final that afternoon to seal the Double. So we were anticipating he would be in a good mood.

He didn't disappoint. He had clearly been celebrating fairly enthusiastically already and he wasn't in the mood to slow down now he was with his England mates. I went to bed reasonably early because we were flying to Beijing the next morning. When I got up, Gazza was still in the bar. It was obvious he hadn't been to bed.

Gazza wasn't a good flyer. He hated flying. So even if he hadn't had a Double to celebrate, he probably would have had a few drinks to prepare himself for the journey anyway. By the time we boarded the plane, we might not have actually left the ground but he was already flying.

On the plane we took the seats that had been assigned to us. I noticed straight away that he was sitting next to Gareth Southgate. They were a couple of rows in front and Gareth looked around at one point and caught my eye. His expression was basically saying, 'Please, no.' He knew he had Gazza for twelve hours non-stop. I was laughing my head off.

The thing with Gazza was that he didn't sleep on planes. Actually, he appeared not to sleep at all. He was a live wire. In fact, he was the livest wire I have ever come across. He just didn't stop. Ever. I don't know when he did sleep. He wasn't one of those guys who suddenly conk out. I don't think I've ever seen him asleep. I dread to think how little rest he got.

We were still on the tarmac when he started asking the steward for a beer. The steward brought him one. No problem. Gazza drank it. He asked the steward for another beer. The steward didn't hear him, so Gazza tugged at his jacket and asked him again. I noticed that the steward gave him a long stare. But he brought him another beer.

Soon after take-off, Gazza asked the steward for another. The steward didn't hear him at first. He was trying to serve other people, too. After a while the steward brought the beer. Not long after that, while he was attending to another passenger, Gazza patted him on the backside and without saying a word, the steward turned round and punched him in the face.

It was a very clever punch. The steward looked around to see who was watching, saw that he had pretty much a free run at it and then clocked him. There was steam coming out of the steward's ears by that stage. He had had enough of it and so he dealt with it and walked off.

Steve McManaman and Robbie Fowler were in the two seats behind Gazza and when they heard the commotion, they popped up like a couple of meerkats. They sensed a bit of mischief, so they were winding Gazza up and telling him he couldn't just take it and that he'd have to give the steward a slap back if honour was to be satisfied.

Gazza was a bit teary. His lip was quivering. He was saying that if his mate Jimmy 'Five Bellies' Gardner was there, the steward would get a smack as well. Gareth was looking back at me again with pleading eyes. Jack Wiseman from the FA and the pilot and the steward all came down and everything started getting a bit out of hand. Gazza was crying and complaining and everybody else was joining in and trying to establish what had happened and what to do about it.

The pilot said that if things did not calm down, he would have to land the plane in Moscow and dump Gazza off the plane there. That made Gazza cry even more. I think they were bluffing. Moscow sounded dramatic, too. I think it was intended to put the fear of God into Gazza and eventually it did the trick and he quietened down.

That was just the flight out.

*   *   *

Things were fairly routine in Beijing. I asked if anybody fancied going into the city to do some sightseeing and have a look at Tiananmen Square one evening. There weren't a lot of takers. Gareth and I were the sum total. You stand out by doing something like that and generally people don't want to stand out when they are in a team environment off the pitch. They want to blend in.

For most of the lads, the preference would be to go out and have a few drinks. I remember back in the summer of 1991, when we were in New Zealand on an England tour when Graham Taylor was boss, *Les Misérables* was on at the theatre across the road from our team hotel in Auckland. I went along with Tony Coton, Keith Curle and Nigel Clough. After a couple of minutes, Tony and Keith got up and left. We did all visit the Great Wall of China on that trip before Euro 96, but I think that was one where the players weren't given a choice.

I didn't play in the match but we beat China 3–0. Nick Barmby scored a couple and Gazza got the third. The shenanigans on the plane didn't seem to have done him an awful lot of harm. But he wasn't done yet. Not by a long chalk.

I love Gazza. I always have done. And during the period last summer when Euro 2020 was postponed because of the pandemic and everybody was watching reruns of Euro 96, it was great to see people being reminded that he was an awful lot more than a court jester. He is the best player this country has produced since Sir Bobby Charlton.

The first time I really became aware of him was when he broke into the first team at Newcastle. I was nowhere near him in terms of talent, but we played a lot of England games together. I made my debut in May 1987 and he made his in September 1988. Neither of us was on the losing side for an England team on many occasions. So I was acutely aware of just how brilliant he was. And I don't use that word lightly. Where did he rank in terms of best British footballers of our generation? Number one. Number one without a doubt. He ticked every box: pure arrogance on a football pitch, not being fazed by any of the opposition he came up against, energy, creativity, vision, technical ability.

There are other players in that conversation, of course. I'd put Peter Shilton in there. To keep your place in the England team for a couple of decades when there was a lot of talented competition and to be that good for that long puts Shilts up there with the best we have had in this country. I'd have Gary Lineker right up there, too. He did it for a whole series of clubs and he scored goals at the very highest level.

Bryan Robson would probably be Gazza's closest rival in my book. Robson had the biggest heart of any player I've played with. He was the complete box-to-box midfielder, a courageous tackler, a relentless runner, great in the air, somebody who did the dirty work as well as grabbing the glory, a man who was dedicated to the team ethic most of all.

Bryan was unlucky at World Cups. He made a big impact at the start of the 1982 tournament, but he had to leave both 1986 and 1990 with injuries, so perhaps he never quite got the stand-out moment he deserved. At club level, he carried Manchester United on his shoulders in the days before they became a dominant force under Sir Alex Ferguson.

I sometimes feel Bryan didn't get the credit he deserved. He played for United at a time when Liverpool were winning trophies, but he dominated their team in the way that Steven Gerrard dominated the Liverpool side when they were in United's shadow.

Gerrard and Frank Lampard were superb players, of course. Gerrard was a fearsome striker of the ball and a beautiful passer, and even if he didn't win the title with Liverpool, he led them to that famous Champions League victory over AC Milan in Istanbul in 2005. It is a measure of Lampard's standing that he became Chelsea's leading all-time scorer playing in midfield.

And Paul Scholes, David Beckham and Wayne Rooney, too. But one of the biggest differences between them and Gazza was that Gazza was able to perform on the biggest stage for England. None of the others were synonymous with a tournament. Gazza was synonymous with two.

The rest of those names I have mentioned were all tainted, to some extent, by being labelled as part of the Golden Generation. And even though that was initially meant as a compliment, it soon became a millstone around their necks. It was used as shorthand for a feeling that they had underachieved and had, in some cases, been carried away with image over substance.

That is one of the ironies around Gazza. There was so much speculation about his personal life, his 'refuelling' habits, going out for kebabs, drinking in working men's clubs, and all the rest of it. But at the end of it all, Gazza lived and breathed football. It was really all he cared about. And for whatever reason, when the big tournaments came around and others faded, Gazza sparkled like a diamond.

Wayne Rooney had some of Gazza's talent, but he didn't have the impact at tournaments he should have done. He has achieved a lot in terms of records for goalscoring and appearances, and he was a fabulous player, but there should have been more to show for that longevity. I was alongside him in South Africa in 2010 when I was part of Fabio Capello's coaching team and Wayne had a really disappointing tournament.

In contrast, Gazza will be remembered for what he did at major tournaments, in 1990 and 1996, and that's when it counts. The bits in between were pretty good as well, although they were affected by injuries. Gazza was the star of the show at the 1990 World Cup and dredged up the best of what was left at Euro 96. He shone at both tournaments.

When people ask why England weren't successful at certain times and why the Golden Generation fell short, I point to the fact that there was only one Gascoigne and no one replicated him. People talk about Gerrard and Scholes, and of course I accept they were fine players, but no one had the ability to light up a tournament like Gazza did.

Maybe my opinion is weighted towards Gazza because I value playing for England so highly. I have always seen the importance of international football. To my mind, nothing replicates what you do when you wear an international jersey. Whatever you do internationally, I put it on a higher stage than club football.

I know a lot of players don't have that mentality any more, so I find it refreshing when England players do come through and value wearing an international shirt. Maybe some players rate the Champions League higher than international football. I'm a different generation, I know, but I don't agree with that.

My reason for saying that is this: 300,000 people at Luton Airport to welcome back World Cup semi-finalists in 1990, and the spirit around the country during Euro 96 when it united us as a nation more than anything I've experienced apart from the London Olympics in 2012.

No single club could set this country alight like eleven Englishmen winning a World Cup or European Championship. I have seen glimpses of it in my time when we have gone to the brink of winning something and fallen just short. We saw the same fervour again in 2018 with the viewing figures for England matches in Russia. So I'm not convinced about the club scenario being more important.

Gazza and I were like chalk and cheese. I only wanted to see the Clown Prince when we were out on the pitch. That was the only time I wanted him alongside me, because if we weren't playing and I found myself anywhere near him, I knew that trouble or mischief of some sort wouldn't be far away.

I wonder if some people hear the stories about Gazza and think he was an irritant, but that wasn't the way it was at all. It was impossible not to love him. He was the same with everybody; he mixed with everybody; he was kind and generous to everybody; he made everybody laugh; he played jokes on everybody.

I was alone in my room at Burnham Beeches one afternoon, putting my boots on the windowsill to dry them off, and I turned around and there was someone wearing an old man's mask. It was like something out of a horror film. It made me jump out of my skin. It was Gazza, of course. He had crept up behind me. I was so startled I very nearly decked him before I realised who it was. He was delighted with how much of a fright he'd given me.

I still see him from time to time. He and I and Tony Adams were lined up to do a few shows before the Euros if they had taken place as planned in the summer of 2020. *An Audience With . . .* You know the kind of thing. I've done that sort of show with Gazza before. Funnily enough, he tends to be the centre of attention. People want to talk to him more than they want to talk to anybody else. He still has that dynamism about him. People still love him.

Some people made fun of him when he turned up and tried to help that guy Raoul Moat, who was wanted for murder and was surrounded by police up in Northumberland in 2010. During the stand-off, Gazza travelled to the scene in his dressing gown with a fishing rod and a cooked chicken and offered to talk to Moat. The police sent him away.

It turned out Gazza was on a pretty serious bender, but it was still typical of him. He would do anything to help anybody. On that particular occasion, he saw somebody he wanted to help, even though he was vulnerable, too. That was the level of kindness he had. It was built into his personality.

When he was in his prime and earning big money, I heard a lot of stories about him taking his family and friends on holiday at the end of the season, paying every bill for every member of the family, rooms, meals, drinks, the whole lot. He earned a lot of money, but I think he gave most of it away.

Plenty of footballers are like that. Because of the way the game is, a lot of players come from disadvantaged backgrounds and their friends and family have never had access to nice hotels or business-class travel or posh restaurants. It is inevitable that a lot of players want to make up for lost time when the money starts coming in.

Maybe they buy watches or fancy cars or both. Often they lavish generosity on their friends and family. Sometimes, that can mean quite an extended family. And even though people like Gazza earn a lot, when you are shouldering all-expenses-paid treats for so many people, that money can disappear pretty quickly.

His kindness and generosity never ceased to amaze me. A month or so before Euro 96, we had my testimonial at the City Ground between Forest and Newcastle United. Gazza was at Rangers by then, but I asked him if he could get me a Lazio shirt for an auction. He pulled this diary out and I have never seen so much scribble on one double page. He wrote a note to remind himself about the shirt and I thought never in a million years was he going to remember.

A couple of months later, Jimmy Five Bellies rang me and said Gazza had got the shirt. That's Paul for you. He is so caring about others that he'll give his last penny to someone. Everyone would talk affectionately about him. The sad thing is that he was a cash cow for some people. He had an army of hangers-on, B-listers who wanted to be seen with him because they knew it would bring them publicity and get their picture in the paper.

People like that, it suited them if Gazza got into a bit of trouble because then there was more chance they'd get mentioned as being out with him. They wanted the reflected glory of being seen with him, because he was such a shining star at the time. Some footballers can see people like that coming and they avoid them. With Gazza, even if he did see them coming, he was too warm-hearted to push them away.

He was in the mould of someone like Alex Higgins or George Best. He was a genius and he wanted to please everybody. It wasn't enough for him to bring so much pleasure to people by what he did on the pitch, even though some of the stuff he did still burns bright in the minds of football fans now.

Think about how large he looms in English football still. His tears in Turin, the contribution he made to that 1990 World Cup, his floated free kick to David Platt, both the through balls that led to Gary Lineker's penalties against Cameroon, the Cruyff Turn against Holland in the group games and everything that he contributed at Euro 96.

But that wasn't enough for him. He wasn't able to detach himself the way other great sportsmen could. It is enough for me to play the game and then move on and be self-contained. But when he came off the pitch, Gazza was still desperate to keep pleasing people. He wanted to make people laugh. He wanted them to like him. He wanted to be the centre of attention.

I'm not a psychologist, but I think he was probably a bit scared of being by himself. He wasn't very good in his own company. He constantly wanted to please people, whether by getting behind the wheel of the team coach at Middlesbrough or giving ridiculous television interviews or pulling funny faces to the camera. Bobby Robson once called him 'as daft as a brush', and that was about right, but he was a clown with a heart of gold.

The amount of foolery he would get up to was limitless. When we first arrived in Sardinia before the 1990 World Cup, Bobby Robson sat the squad down and told us that the preservation of energy was vitally important. That was his central message. He wanted it to be one of our ruling thoughts as the tournament progressed.

Now, the Is Molas hotel was not restricted to just the England team when we were staying there. There were members of the public, too. One day, we were sitting by the swimming pool and there was a commotion on the left-hand side. Gazza had stripped naked and mummified himself in toilet roll and he was standing on the diving board. He launched himself in and swam a length and came up naked and then walked off through the tourists, laughing.

That was almost normal. The day before the World Cup semi-final in Turin, he famously got involved in a tennis match against a couple of Americans at our hotel there. I was told it went to five sets. So much for preserving energy. Chris Waddle, who was his room-mate, always did his best to cover for him, but this time Bobby found out about it. He got us all together, stared at Gazza and said, 'Gentlemen, there is an idiot amongst us.'

Up until the semi-final, there had been a lot of security around the team and it was really just the players and the support staff in our own bubble. After the semi-final, things changed and a few friends and family members hung around with us in Bari while we were waiting to play the third-place play-off.

We were having a meal at the hotel one night and Gazza's mate Jimmy Five Bellies was there. I liked Jimmy. He got a bad press but he was a decent bloke and he was devoted to Gazza. He would do anything for him. Anyway, I was eating my meal, minding my own business, still trying to come to terms with everything that had happened in Turin, when Gazza came bounding up to the table and asked me if I would do him a favour.

I nodded. He said, 'Could you punch Jimmy in the face for me?' I said I wasn't going to do that. 'It's all right,' Gazza said. 'He doesn't mind.' I said I still wouldn't do it. So Gazza dragged

Jimmy over to the table and punched him in the face himself. Then he asked me to do it again.

'It's all right, Pearcey,' Jimmy said. 'I don't mind. It'd be brilliant if you could.'

I told them to get lost, so Gazza started dragging Jimmy round to other tables in the dining room and asking people if they would punch Jimmy in the face. To this day, I have absolutely no idea what they were up to.

I didn't see Gazza's problems at that time. A few years later, when Graham Taylor was England manager, he talked about Gazza's 'refuelling habits' between games and everyone assumed it was a loaded reference to drinking. 'I cannot bring myself to publicly record what all of his problems are,' Graham said back then, 'otherwise all Hell would break loose, and what I find difficult is that there are people who know but want me or someone else to say it for them, and I will not go all of the way down that line.'

Even by 1996, I wasn't aware that he had a drink problem. Maybe I just didn't look closely enough. Maybe I didn't want to. We all knew he liked a drink and went to extremes, but the culture was different then. It wasn't uncommon for the England squad to go out while on England duty. When I first broke into the squad, there would always be a group of lads who would go to a place called Skindles in Maidenhead to have a few drinks.

I didn't look at Gazza and think he was an excessive drinker who had problems. I thought he was a funny fella who enjoyed a drink and a laugh. He blended into the mix, even if he was an eccentric and extreme version of the rest of us. I didn't have alarm bells ringing. The press boys were the same.

When Graham Taylor took over the squad after the 1990 World Cup, he took everyone out to the theatre to watch the Buddy Holly musical, and then after it was over, he took us on to a private room in a hotel for some karaoke. It was Graham's first international get-together. Graham and Gazza brought the house down by singing a version of 'It's Raining Men' and they were pouring jugs of water over each other. I was sitting there thinking, 'Well, this is going to be an interesting few years.' It was difficult for managers. They had to rein him in, but they also had to encourage him.

Many years later, just before he died, Graham wrote about some of the issues being Gazza's manager brought up. 'I could phone him four, five or six times without getting through,' Graham wrote. 'I'd leave messages with his brother or his friends or whoever it was he was with. At one point he was worried that journalists might ring him, impersonating people he knew, so we had a code-word system. At one stage the code word was "Kevin Brock" – the name of a Newcastle United midfielder. It was quite bizarre at times.'

Bobby Robson and Terry Venables both managed to get the best out of him. They gave him just enough rope but not too much. I loved his attitude to the game itself. We were the same on the training pitch. I liked to train the way I played. Gazza loved to train, even if there was a level of stupidity underpinning certain things he did on the pitch. But he loved to train. And he was usually the last person off the training pitch, because he loved football. We mirrored each other in that way. But with regard to his eating habits, his sleeping habits – I didn't want him anywhere near me in any preparation. He was so hyperactive. If you roomed with him, he had to have the light on all night.

He was an enigma but, my God, he unified the squad. Everybody loved the fella. He had a heart of gold. Everyone loved him to bits. And you knew his worth as a player. I was an also-ran in some ways, but Gazza was an artist in what he did. But if he was going out for a drink, I didn't want to be there because it wouldn't be a quiet night.

You want to look after Gazza. He's that kind of bloke. I feel so protective towards him, it's incredible. I feel so emotionally involved with him because of his vulnerability and because of the history we share. I know the good times we have had together. Some of those tournaments, he lit them up for me. I didn't see his vulnerability when he was playing, I'm afraid. I just saw someone who wanted to make people smile.

He was happy-go-lucky and he was everyone's friend, but somewhere down the line he needed solid influences behind him, which he probably didn't have. There was no one there to turn around and say, 'Gazza, no, stop. Your career is too important for that.' But at the time, none of us thought about his fragility. We just thought he was our Clown Prince. In the end, it caught up with him before the 1998 World Cup, when Glenn Hoddle became so concerned about his behaviour and his fitness that he left him out of his squad.

I felt for Gazza when I heard about that because I knew how devastated he must have been. There were reports from Spain of how he reacted when Glenn broke the news to him. He never played for England again after that. His last cap ended up being a friendly against Belgium a few days before the World Cup began.

He was the main creative influence in the 1990 side and it was the same in 1996. In fact, he was the biggest creative influence in

English football in maybe fifty years. There have been some great players to wear an England shirt, but in my view, he had the lot. He is a stand-out. It's hard to overstate his influence. He made everyone relaxed, for one thing.

If you are looking at a team-mate and thinking he's worried about the opposition, it can be unnerving. When you looked at Gazza, you saw a player who was thinking, 'Don't worry, I'll set the game alight, no problem.' When Bobby Robson tried to tell him about the Dutch team we were playing in the group stages in 1990 and how good they were, Gazza said, 'Don't worry about them, just give me the ball.' It wasn't bravado. He meant it.

After playing China, we flew to Hong Kong. I knew things were going to get lively. We played against a Hong Kong Select XI on 26 May and after the game Gazza said we all had to go out because it was his birthday and he wanted the whole squad to celebrate with him. It turned out his birthday was actually the next day, but technically, I suppose, once it got past midnight, he was telling the truth. And he was definitely planning on going past midnight. A lot of the boys started making plans. A few of us decided against it.

I was rooming with Steve Stone, who was a young Forest player starting to make his way in the game. I gave him a long talk about how I didn't think it was a good idea to go out. I went on about my experience in the game and what I'd learned and told him it would be a good night to stay back at the hotel and have a quiet one.

'If you want to take my advice,' I said, 'I've been around the scene for a while, Gazza's going out, the media will be out looking for stories, they'll be looking to trip people up, Gazza will be holding court, my advice is stay in tonight and give it a miss. We've got a big tournament coming up.'

I told him there would be a lot of photographers around and that it would be easy to get sucked into bad publicity, which was the last thing he needed at this stage of his career. It was a proper lecture that I liked to think carried a lot of gravitas.

Stoney looked at me when I had finished, then said, 'Don't worry, I won't wake you when I get in.'

There were a few of us who resisted Gazza's entreaties and decided not to go out. Tony Adams was one. He knew himself too well to get involved in something in the public glare. I just knew it would be a disaster. Gareth Southgate asked me what I thought and he, at least, heeded my advice. I think the Neville brothers decided against it, too. It was one of the better decisions I made as an England player.

The players found their way to the China Jump club in Causeway Bay, rather the worse for wear. And pictures of them ended up splashed all over the front pages of the tabloids. They weren't pretty. A lot of the lads, including Gazza, obviously, were drenched in booze, with their shirts ripped, standing around laughing as spirits were poured down the throats of people sitting in the Dentist's Chair.

The Dentist's Chair was, well, a dentist's chair. You sat back in it while the bar staff poured drink down you. I think a few of the lads took part in that particular ritual. Steve Stone, by the way, had a lucky escape. He told me that in one of the pictures that appeared in the papers of all the lads in a row, he had been cropped off the end.

The rest of them got it between the eyes. Particularly Gazza.

The Sun's front-page headline was 'Disgracefool' and there was general dismay at home that the players could have acted like that so close to the tournament. I realised it had been a big night when I came down for breakfast the next morning, but I didn't realise quite how big until I saw the pictures.

Things got even worse on the Cathay Pacific flight back to England. I was aware that some of the boys were involved in a card school, but things got a bit out of hand. High jinks, whatever you want to call it. I wasn't sitting in the same section of the plane, so I didn't actually see what happened. I've heard the same stories as you – a player being put in an overhead locker – but I'm not sure that actually happened.

What did happen was that some of the fold-out television screens that you get on planes were kicked off their hinges in the middle of a melee. The damage that was done was also made public when we got back and there was a general blood lust for individuals to be punished. Gazza appeared to be central to most of the mischief and there were calls for him to be banished from the squad.

Terry Venables dealt with it masterfully. Our tournament could have disintegrated there and then. It could have foundered on divisions and backbiting and people trying to cover themselves and looking after number one. Terry didn't let that happen. Instead, he made sure we made a positive out of the negative. He made sure the adversity brought us closer together.

We had a team meeting at Burnham Beeches and Terry said he wanted us all to take 'collective responsibility' for what had happened on the plane, even though he knew that most of the players hadn't been involved. He wanted us all to contribute £5,000 for the damage to the plane, stick together and move on.

He knew sections of the media were baying for Gazza's blood and he was determined not to pander to them.

I wasn't too pleased about the £5,000. Neither was my ex-wife. I'd flown to the Far East and back, had a few early nights and slept on the plane home. Stumping up five grand because someone else had caused a spot of grief seemed a bit steep, particularly when I saw the pictures of what the boys had got up to in the China Jump. I may have muttered a few oaths under my breath at that team meeting.

I was a different animal when it came to club football and international football. In club football, I could see the advantage of an odd binge to bring the lads together. In international football, I always thought you had to be the ultimate professional. What had happened in Hong Kong and on the plane didn't sit well with me. Maybe it was to do with my upbringing as an electrician and what it meant to represent England.

But the fact that Gazza was largely responsible for both things took the sting out of it all for me immediately. If I was going to give anyone any tolerance, it was him. I felt protective of him then, just as I do now. You can't be cross with him for long. And, anyway, there was no point in one person standing up and saying I'm not getting involved in this.

Gazza just didn't have an off-switch. Even after we had got back from Hong Kong, he was irrepressible. Terry had said we could have a few drinks in the bar at Burnham Beeches if we wanted to and, by that time, there was a media marquee at the far end of the hotel garden where all the television interviews were conducted during Euro 96.

The television lights were on and it was obvious Terry was doing some sort of media interview in there, probably having to fend off more questions about what had gone on in Hong Kong and on the plane. We were watching Terry talking on the big screen in the bar and we could see the lights of the hotel, where we were sitting, in the background.

Gradually, you could see this figure running from the direction of the hotel towards the camera, behind Terry. He got closer and closer and it looked as if he wasn't wearing any clothes, but nobody could have known who it was because he had a shirt wrapped around his head. We knew who it was. The players were lying on the floor, crying with laughter.

There was another way of looking at that fine we all had to pay for the damage: Gazza's ability paid that £5,000 fine back with some win bonuses. And the principle of collective responsibility was a master stroke by Terry. It galvanised the team and bonded us together. Without it, there could have been divisions and splits and rancour.

If you want to know whether Terry got it right or not, all you need to do is look at the way Gazza performed at Euro 96. He was the star of the show.

Later in the tournament, Gazza scored his famous goal against Scotland. You can trace that back to Terry's decision about collective responsibility, too. Terry knew the media were looking for a sacrificial lamb, but he wouldn't give them one. Gazza owed him after that. And probably one or two other players did as well.

Gazza repaid him in bundles.

5

IN MY STADIUM OF GOOD AND EVEL

WE KNEW WE were under a massive cloud when we got back from Hong Kong and set up camp at Burnham Beeches. We had the meeting about collective responsibility soon after our return and, for all the defiance that came with that, we all knew we had brought some of the pressure that we were now feeling upon ourselves. Euro 96 was only a few days away and we knew that the public was wondering what the hell was going on.

We were fourth favourites for the tournament, behind Holland, Italy and Germany. I understood why so many people fancied the Dutch to win. They didn't have quite the same level of superstar player as at the 1990 World Cup, but they had Dennis Bergkamp in attack and Clarence Seedorf in the centre of midfield. Danny Blind anchored their defence and was a player I admired, and even though Patrick Kluivert was only 19, he had already scored the winner in the 1995 Champions League final for Ajax. There were some worries about him being injured, but it was clear he was a superstar in the making. They had other good players dotted around the side and a lot of people thought this might be the tournament in which they finally made their talent pay off.

Italy had a fine side, too. They had Paolo Maldini and Alessandro Costacurta at the heart of their defence, for a start, two of the all-time great defenders. And they had three players in attack who would give any defender like me pause for thought. Alessandro Del Piero, Gianfranco Zola and Pierluigi Casiraghi were three forwards of real quality. Italy had got to the World Cup final two years earlier in the USA. We thought they would be a really tough team to beat.

And then, of course, there was Germany. Perhaps they didn't have quite the star quality of some Germany teams but everyone knew you would have to go a long way before you got a bad Germany team at a tournament. They were a unified country now as well, so they had an even bigger pool of players they could choose from.

Not least among those was Matthias Sammer. He had played for East Germany until 1990 and he was a huge addition to a Germany side that was mainly made up of players from the former West Germany. He would have been a huge addition to any international team.

He was a superb defensive midfielder. As it turned out, he was probably the best player at the tournament. Again, he might not have had quite the star quality of someone like Lothar Matthäus, but that didn't make him any less effective. He ran that Germany side and we knew that they would be contenders. They almost always were.

They had a solid defence and their midfield was packed with clever players like Mehmet Scholl and Dieter Eilts. Jürgen Klinsmann was their skipper and he was still an excellent forward. They were not spectacular but they were solid and organised and technically excellent. They didn't carry the air of

Playing for England has been the proudest achievement of my life in football.

Bryan Robson's injury against the Dutch compounded a torrid start to our 1990 World Cup.

David Platt's last-gasp winner against Belgium in Bologna left us within two victories of the final.

Des Walker had Rudi Völler in his pocket in our hard-fought semi-final against West Germany.

Gary Lineker warned the England bench of Paul Gascoigne's distress over his booking in extra time.

I smashed my penalty down the middle but the ball flew to safety off Bodo Illgner.

Devastated after seeing my kick saved, I was in a trance of misery and frustration.

Lothar Matthäus showed class by consoling Chris Waddle after his spot-kick failure.

Peter Shilton was unable to save one of the West Germans' five textbook penalties in Turin.

Striding out behind managers Brian Clough and Terry Venables before the 1991 FA Cup final.

Celebrating with friend and 'rival' Graeme Le Saux after his 1995 goal against Brazil.

After twelve barren games, Alan Shearer began Euro 96 by scoring in the first match, against Switzerland.

I could hardly avoid Marco Grassi's lob, but the ensuing penalty earned the Swiss a draw.

My second-half replacement, Jamie Redknapp, helped turn the game against Scotland.

Tony Adams's ball-winning was renowned but he also proved a true leader at Euro 96.

Gazza confounded Scotland's Colin Hendry before beating his Rangers colleague Andy Goram: 2–0.

The 'Dentist's Chair' routine greeted Paul's euphoric goal, harking back to Hong Kong.

Shirtless but happy and relieved with David Seaman after we saw off the Scots.

Steve McManaman in full flight against the Netherlands in our final group match.

Teddy Sheringham's header doubled the Dutch deficit after Alan Shearer's penalty.

Alan scored emphatically, à la Carlos Alberto, after Teddy's deft, Pelé-style lay-off.

Teddy pounced again to put us 4–0 up and cruising against one of
the Euro 96 favourites.

greatness that West Germany had done at the 1990 World Cup, but they were still a formidable unit.

We didn't know it then but France were only two years away from winning the World Cup and their boss, Aimé Jacquet, was putting all the building blocks in place for the side that would go on to win on home soil in 1998. Any team with Marcel Desailly and Laurent Blanc at its heart and Zinedine Zidane beginning to exert his genius is going to have a chance.

France had Didier Deschamps sitting in the heart of midfield and Youri Djorkaeff complementing Zidane in midfield, just as he would two years later. By Euro 96, maverick influences like David Ginola and Eric Cantona had been removed from the picture and the team was on the brink of a sustained spell of success that is still going on to this day.

There were some decent underdogs in the tournament, too. Few thought the Czech Republic would do quite as well as they did, but their midfielder Pavel Nedvěd was one of the best players of his generation. Karel Poborsky and Patrik Berger had such good tournaments that their performances earned them moves to the Premier League, with Manchester United and Liverpool respectively.

So there were plenty of opponents for us to be respectful of. I thought we had the talent to go all the way, but I knew that the mood music probably didn't sound particularly tuneful as we went into our first game.

All sorts of things contributed to that: we hadn't really been able to show any consistent form in the run-up to the tournament; people were fretting about the Christmas Tree and what formation we were going to play; we'd battered an aeroplane and been out on the lash and got our pictures splashed all over the front pages.

So much for going to the Far East to keep out of trouble. We had flown smack bang into the middle of it and got bumped and thrown around just as we would have done if we'd been thrown into an electrical storm. Sure, there were no hooliganism problems. Not from the fans, anyway. But we'd still managed to put football on the front pages for the wrong reasons.

Even on the eve of the tournament, there were still worries about crowd trouble. We had become so conditioned to hooliganism issues during the 1980s and early 1990s that no one could quite believe they would not recur at a home tournament. It was as if we had become so conditioned to trouble we were bracing ourselves for more.

There was a lot of anticipation about the tournament and the fact that the England team was playing in one at home for the first time since 1966, but there was also a great deal of apprehension: not just about whether we could live up to expectations on the pitch but about whether we could actually stage a jamboree like this without embarrassing ourselves.

Someone from the Met Police came to the hotel and gave the team a presentation on football hooliganism. I didn't quite see what beneficial effect it was going to have for the players, to be honest. There were knives and axes and machetes that had been confiscated from football fans laid out all over the lounge at Burnham Beeches. I don't know what the point of that was.

I've mentioned already the way England fans were described by our own sports minister during the 1990 World Cup. This time we were also worried at a basic level about wider issues like infrastructure and our transport system and our stadiums and our organisation, and whether we would be able to look back on the Euros with pride.

Things are very different now. We have staged a whole series of huge events in this country in the last twenty years, but in 1996 there hadn't been anything for a long time. No Olympic Games since 1948, no Commonwealth Games since 1934, no World Cup since 1966, no Cricket World Cup since 1983, no World Athletics Championships ever, no European Championship in football ever.

As the host nation, you have extra pressure on you on the pitch, whether you like it or not. And you have to win the crowd over. We look back now with rose-tinted glasses and assume the fans were brilliant from the first moment to the last at Euro 96, but it was never like that. All we remember is the performance against Holland and how unlucky we were against Germany, but a lot of the games weren't great, either. In the end, we were swept along by the emotion, but there was a lot of dross.

Before the tournament, I thought we had more chance of winning than we had done in 1990. We had a very good team. I'm not sure the team in 1990, looking back, was a great side, though we had some very good individuals and, most of all, we had Gazza when he was young and fearless and brilliant and the best midfielder in the world.

When you watch some of the games we played in 1990 now, there were some really, really poor performances. The Cameroon game was on television recently as part of the nostalgia we were all wallowing in during the lockdown and I couldn't believe how bad we were. I was really embarrassed. Some of the defending was awful, both mine and the team's. It was incredible to watch.

I felt we had a more hard-nosed team of leaders in 1996, a more rounded team. I think there was a better squad in 1990, but the eleven or twelve in 1996 was a better line-up. We really felt we could go toe-to-toe with the Germans at the Euros. Six years earlier, we thought things would have to conspire in our favour for us to be victorious.

Burnham Beeches was a good base. It was a smallish hotel and we had it all to ourselves. It was in a great location, too, near to the M40 but in the Buckinghamshire countryside. It was close enough to Wembley for it to be an easy journey in by coach, but it was far enough away to feel removed from the mania that was starting to grip the country.

It was a time before Netflix and box sets, so watching films was still a communal experience and that was mainly how I used to spend any down time I had in the evenings. There weren't that many films on the television but companies used to send us videos, so a group of five or six of us would settle down after dinner to watch a film. Doc Crane loved a cowboy film, so I became a bit of an expert on John Wayne movies. He was one of Sir Alex Ferguson's favourites, too. If you think that was square, I'd also spend a portion of the afternoons having the tea and scones I mentioned in the hotel lounge. All very traditional.

Once we were locked down within the tournament, the players were leading a lifestyle that was fairly monastic. I couldn't tell you what Gazza was doing, apart from scaring the hell out of me, but for the rest of the boys, the tournament meant too much to be going wild. The games come thick and fast. If you are not living right, it finds you out. A lot of sports people are bingers.

They go and get drunk, relieve a bit of pressure and then it's back to the grindstone again, but at a tournament there isn't enough recovery time for that kind of behaviour. Maybe it's why some players find the rhythms of being away so difficult.

We were due to open our tournament against Switzerland on a Saturday afternoon at 3 p.m. There were just a few people littered around the car park at Burnham Beeches when we wandered out to get on the coach and a few more waiting outside the gates, but as the tournament went on, those numbers swelled and swelled until, by the later stages, there were cars following us down the motorway with flags flying out of the windows.

I've played in away matches where there have been scenes like that. I played for England in Turkey in 1991 when we were met by Turkish fans at the airport making throat-slitting gestures and following us down the motorway in their cars blaring their horns. By the end of Euro 96, the mania in the country was approaching those sorts of levels.

For now, though, it was relatively subdued. It was tense, most of all. There was anticipation but there was fear, too. It was about nerves. The first game of the tournament, the mentality is always that you cannot lose. If you lose the first game of a three-game group, you are in trouble. It is more important not to lose than to win.

As Euro 96 wore on, home advantage played a massive part in our favour, but at the start of the tournament, I'm not sure it did. Because of the lead-in to the tournament – the pressure in the media beforehand, the results, the performances – everything was loaded on us.

Still, I always loved the journey into Wembley. In those days of the old Wembley, the coach would make its way slowly up Wembley Way towards the Twin Towers and it felt like you were at one with the fans. You could see the excitement on their faces, the way they were urging you on, how much it meant to them, as well as how much it meant to you.

I was very much a routine person. I sat in the same place on the coach as I sat on our way to training. I was next to Gareth, but for games of that magnitude, I wasn't the chattiest of travelling companions. I just wanted to be in my own world, concentrating on the game and what lay ahead.

It meant a lot to me, playing at Wembley. I had a lot of history with the place. Because my family had moved from Shepherd's Bush to Kingsbury when I was five, for me Wembley was not some Holy Grail in the south of England you go to once in a lifetime. It was a couple of stops away on the Jubilee Line. It was a local landmark. It was a place that was part of my daily life.

It was one of the reasons why I made the private decision to retire from international football after the Euros. I thought that there could be no better way to go out than playing for England in a tournament on home soil, at a stadium you loved and in the borough where you grew up.

I was 34 in 1996. I was getting on. In two years, I would be 36 and trying to make it to a major tournament, playing in a position where you were being asked to be more and more mobile. I wasn't sure whether I was going to make that. It felt like the right time. I thought if I didn't make that call, the next manager would make it for me.

Anyway, when I became an electrician as a teenager, I went past the stadium every day on the number 83 bus that crawled through the traffic past Wembley Park station. And when I was 14, a friend of mine who was a porter at the stadium, working in the bars, getting the pies and hot dogs from the storerooms and bringing them to the concourses, said that he could get me a part-time job there.

So I worked there in the 1970s at England games for a bit of spending money. I worked behind the bars on the concourse, bringing the trolley round and stocking things up. It was a good opportunity for me to see the games as well. I'd catch a glimpse if I was going round the concourse. I'd nip up the stairs that led to the aisles occasionally to have a peek at the action.

I was also a ballboy there for the FA Vase between Sheffield FC and Billericay Town in 1977 and later, when I was playing non-league for Wealdstone, I used to go to the greyhound racing there on Friday nights. There was a dog track that ran around the outside of the pitch. I knew all my mates were down the local pub, but because I was already so committed to my career, I didn't want to go drinking or be out late, so I went to Wembley dogs.

It was a local sports venue for us as I was growing up. My mum and dad would take me to the greyhound racing on a Bank Holiday Monday and there would be 40,000 people in the crowd. I went to the World Speedway final in 1978 there as well and saw all the top riders of the time, including Ole Olsen and Ivan Mauger.

I was even there in May 1975 when the stunt man Evel Knievel attempted to jump over thirteen London buses. My oldest brother took me and we were there with 90,000 other fans to see him coming down a long and steep yellow slide and flying over the buses. He almost made it, but he didn't quite clear the last bus and he came tumbling off.

He broke a hand, fractured two vertebrae and broke his pelvis. 'I've got to tell you that you are the last people in the world who will ever see me jump, because I will never, ever, ever jump again. I am through,' he told the crowd. He was a big star in those days. I felt like I was part of history.

Maybe people don't remember him now. I suppose a lot of people went to watch him crash. He was famous for crashing, really. I sometimes wonder if there is a similar instinct with fans going to watch their football teams. Most of all they want to see them win, I know, but sometimes, perhaps when things are going wrong and they want a change, it feels like they want to see them crash, too.

So to walk out at Wembley as a player was almost surreal. It wasn't a mystical place to me, because I knew every nook and cranny, but it was a special, special stadium. The walk from the tunnel at one end of the stadium to the halfway line was fantastic. When the FA Cup final was the biggest day of the football year, in the days before the Premier League, watching the players walk across that turf before the game always sent a shiver down my spine.

I feel incredibly privileged to have made that walk many times. It's one of the features the new stadium lacks. There was that explosion of excitement and cheering when the teams emerged and then the slow burn of the march across the turf to where you stood for the anthems. It was pure theatre.

One of the most memorable occasions for that was the 1991 FA Cup final, when Forest played Spurs. It was the match when Gazza sustained the serious knee injury that was to affect him for much of the rest of his career, but it was an amazing moment walking out behind Brian Clough and Terry Venables, the opposing managers, at the head of the Forest team. Brian grabbed Terry's hand midway through and held it as they walked.

There are great things about the generation of new stadiums that we have in football. They are safer, cleaner places for fans to enjoy football, but they are also more sedate than they used to be. Part of that is the all-seater element. But when we walked out that day at Wembley against Switzerland in June 1996, the atmosphere was already rocking.

I had gone through my usual pre-match routine. It never changed. I went in the dressing room, checked my place, checked that my boots and pads were there, checked everything was right. Then I went out on to the pitch to look at the turf and check whether I needed a stud change. Finally I went back into the dressing room and I didn't come out again until kick-off.

I didn't want any surprises. I was very methodical in my preparation. I used to stay in the dressing room to warm up. Everything was on the clock. I had a set routine for club and country. As time went on in football, the longest you were at a stadium was an hour and a half before kick-off for international games. When I first started in club football, it was a bit more casual and you got there at 2 p.m.

At Euro 96, we were there ninety minutes before kick-off. I used to put my boots on and then walk on the pitch. I would get changed forty-five or fifty minutes before kick-off. I would kick the ball against the wall at a set time, stretch with the physio at a set time, have a loosener up and down the dressing room to get blood into the muscles at a set time.

It was a regime that suited me. I don't think Incey went out and warmed up on the pitch, either. But at club level, it was only ever me who stayed in the dressing room for a lot of the time. When I joined Coventry as a kid, the ex-Wolves player Kenny Hibbitt was an old pro there and he never went out to warm up. I asked him why. He said, 'I get paid for an hour and a half. I'm not going to go out and do any more.' I looked at him and laughed, but as my career went on and I got to know what suited me, I followed the same pattern.

My dietary timings were unusual, too. Most players ate three and a quarter hours before kick-off. That was too late for me. I used to like to go in with an empty belly. That partly came from my mother-in-law. She worked with horses – I've seen pictures of her leading Lester Piggott's horse into the parade ring – and she said to me once, 'You'd never feed a horse before a big race.' So I left it five hours between eating and kick-off.

In any case, I never quite understood the sense in going through a warm-up on the pitch. I have never seen a boxer go into the ring before a fight and warm up and then go back to his dressing room. He gets warmed up in his dressing room, does a bit of shadow boxing maybe, but that's it. With me, it was as much a psychological thing as a physical thing and I had a good record of not having too many physical injuries.

I used to look at my team-mates as they came back in after warm-up and they would all be sweating. They had been out in the sun for half an hour warming up and I thought, 'Why would you do that?' It drains your body. I never used to go out. I got in a routine which made me think I was physically more prepared than any of my team-mates and mentally better prepared as well, and when I got out in that tunnel alongside the opposition, I thought of it as the walk to a boxing ring and it worked for me.

There was no sign of the Christmas Tree formation when we were told the team for the game against the Swiss. It was a more familiar set-up, to English eyes anyway. Terry went with a version of 4-4-2, with Gary Neville at right back, Gareth Southgate and Tony Adams in the centre of defence and me on the left. Paul Ince sat in front of the back four and Darren Anderton, Gazza and Steve McManaman made up the rest of the midfield. Teddy Sheringham played off Alan Shearer in attack.

That meant there were six survivors from the starting line-up in Terry's first game in charge, against Denmark in March 1994. It showed that for all his tactical innovation and his ability to trust in different systems, there was consistency in his selections. Time and injury had deprived him of some of his favourites – fortunately for me – but he stayed loyal to most of his selections.

Switzerland were a good side. We knew that. Under Roy Hodgson, they had qualified for the 1994 World Cup – which was more than we had managed – and even though Roy had moved on to Inter Milan, they were still an accomplished team, with several very good technical players. They had Ramon Vega at the heart of their defence, Ciriaco Sforza was a clever midfielder and up front they had Kubilay Türkyilmaz, who played for Grasshopper Zürich, and Stéphane Chapuisat, who didn't actually make the starting line-up for the game against us.

They had not had a great build-up to the tournament but they still fancied their chances against us. They knew the pressure would be on us from the home crowd and they were aware that our preparations had not been as smooth as they might have been.

I saw Vega talking about that recently. 'A week before the game they were having a great time in Hong Kong,' Vega said, 'and we thought maybe they'll be recovering from the hangover, so maybe it would be an opportunity for us to win against these guys. We were preparing that week, thinking we might have a good chance because they'll underestimate us, a small Swiss team, and the way they were acting showed that.'

We felt good going into the game, though. We felt comfortable in our formation and, despite the nerves, we started the game well. I had a shot from the edge of the area that flew high over the bar after Gazza squared it to me. For once, a pass from Gazza was not quite perfect. It was a bit heavy and I had to stretch for the shot. 'Bad ball,' Gazza mouthed at me as we ran back to our positions.

We felt in charge in the opening exchanges. McManaman made a flying start, jinking between two Swiss defenders on the left. Soon after, he had a shot that Marco Pascolo, the Swiss goalkeeper, pushed away and then Gary Neville produced a thundering drive from 20 yards out that the keeper tipped over the crossbar. Gary was only 21 at that tournament, but the way he played in it was an indicator of the career that lay ahead of him.

Midway through the half we took the lead. Incey played a really clever reverse pass through to Shearer. It went through the legs of one Switzerland defender and then eluded the desperate lunge of another, who tried to cut it out. It was perfectly weighted for Alan, who ran on to it and smashed it past Pascolo.

'Well, wouldn't you know it,' Barry Davies said on the BBC commentary. He pointed out that that was the Shearer everyone knew, the Shearer who was a proven goalscorer. Trevor Brooking, who was analysing the game alongside him, pointed out as quietly as he could that Alan was actually offside when the ball was played through to him, but everyone agreed that, given this was supposed to be a homecoming party, it would be best not to mention that too often.

That was a huge boost for us as a team and for Alan in particular. He had gone twenty-one months without scoring for England and even though he was a strong character, he was aware of everyone using that statistic as a stick to beat him with. Strikers like him thrive off goals and when I saw that one fly in off the post like a rocket, I knew it would be a huge boost for our chances in the tournament.

Some people have said that Alan should have squared the ball to Teddy Sheringham, who was unmarked to his left – and was also offside when Incey played the ball – and would have had a tap-in if Alan had played it to him. Alan was never going to do that. I wouldn't expect that thought even to enter the mind of a striker of his quality. Alan knows how well he can strike the ball and he was clean through on goal.

In that situation, even though some people might say it would be the unselfish thing to do to square the ball, I actually think there would be more risk in not shooting. Alan was a deadly finisher and the drought with England hadn't changed that. We needed him to be the scorer and he needed to be the scorer to set himself up for that tournament. It was a clinical strike. He is judged on goals. They defined his career and his life. For us to be successful, Shearer had to be the top scorer in the tournament.

We nearly went further ahead soon afterwards. McManaman was tripped as he ran away from the byline, but as he sprawled on the ground, the referee played the advantage and the ball ran to me. I whipped it over first time and Alan rose unmarked to meet it about ten yards out. It was a high ball, so it was difficult for him to time it correctly and get the power he needed. It bounced just wide of Pascolo's right-hand post.

We had had a lot of the play but the Swiss did not give up. Close to half-time, they made a chance on the right. A ball was played in to the feet of Türkyilmaz and I went with him to close him down. Türkyilmaz was a clever player and he let the ball run at just the right moment to catch me on my heels. He left me for dead. I was nowhere.

He got to the byline and slid the ball across the six-yard box to the back post, where it looked as if there was a queue of Swiss forwards lining up to put it away. Marco Grassi was the one who got the touch but he had to stretch to get there and the ball bobbled just before it reached him. That felt like a sign of deliverance.

The bobble meant that the ball ballooned up off Grassi's shin and even though he was only about two yards out, it hit the underside of the crossbar and bounced down and out. There was a melee in the area but we managed to clear it. It was the same end where Geoff Hurst had hit the bar in the 1966 World Cup final. That time, the ball had crossed the line. This time, it hadn't. The Swiss could not believe it. It was a huge escape for us.

It was a let-off but it seemed to make us nervous. It was a reminder that something might go wrong and spoil the story. Despite that, we still managed one more chance before the interval and could easily have gone 2–0 up. I think a two-goal cushion really would have settled the nerves. One wasn't quite enough.

We had a free kick wide on the right and I swung it over deep towards the back post. Teddy had slipped his marker and he rose to meet it unmarked about six yards out. He did everything right and headed it down, but Pascolo saved it. The ball ricocheted around a bit and when it came back to Teddy, he could not quite get it out of his feet and Pascolo was able to block it again.

After half-time, it was a different story. Switzerland sensed our nerves and came back strongly. Grassi wriggled through our defence and I flung myself at his feet to block his shot when he just had Seaman to beat. Then, in quick succession, the Swiss had a penalty shout turned down and Chapuisat, who had come on midway through the second half, blasted a shot over from the edge of the box.

It was all Switzerland now as we tried to hang on for full time. Tony Adams brought Chapuisat down right on the edge of our box as he was bursting through and was shown the yellow card for it. When the resulting free kick cannoned off the wall, Johann Vogel, who had been one of their best players, shot from the edge of the area and I thought he had scored. The ball seemed to have Dave Seaman beaten. It looked like it was flying inside his left-hand post, but just at the final instant, it curled away and missed the post by inches.

I thought that might be the stroke of luck we needed to get home safely with a narrow victory. But seven minutes from the end, they pumped a long ball forward and Gareth made a bit of a mess of a defensive header. It went straight into the path of Grassi on the edge of the box. I think he saw that Seaman had been caught off his line and tried to lift the ball over him with his left foot. It was more of an attempted lob than a shot.

I'd seen the danger and I was right on top of him when he hit it. I had my right arm raised as I went to challenge Grassi and the ball hit it at point-blank range. There was nothing I could have done, but the referee awarded a penalty. I couldn't believe it. I put my hands on my head. Türkyilmaz took the kick, Seaman dived to his right but Türkyilmaz rolled the ball to his left and the Swiss were level.

Things nearly got worse in the few minutes that were left before the final whistle. Chapuisat twisted Tony Adams out of shape near the byline and when he pulled the ball back for Grassi, his shot was sneaking in at the near post until Dave got down quickly to turn it behind for a corner. In the nervous final seconds, I tried to boot the ball away in the box and missed it before Dave fell on it. When we heard the final whistle go, it was a relief, but we had to admit that the Swiss deserved their point.

At least we hadn't lost. That would have killed us. After so much expectation, to have lost against a team that were perceived as also-rans would have left us damaged psychologically. I think it would have been hard to come back from a defeat in the opening game. So even though we felt annoyed that we had not played well, there was some consolation in getting a point.

As I walked back towards the tunnel, I didn't feel great. If there was one overriding thought in my mind, it was 'Here we go again'. Some of the memories of my last moments at the 1990 World Cup came flooding back, those familiar feelings that I had let people down. It wasn't quite as spectacular, obviously, but in the opening match of our home tournament, I hadn't exactly covered myself in glory.

Most obviously, I had given away the penalty that had allowed the Swiss to equalise. At the back of it all, I knew I wasn't a natural first choice for the manager. The team wasn't playing well enough for me to think that I could put in a bad performance or two and keep my place. It would be fair to say that I was not in my pomp as a player. The better years were slightly behind me, so I was always questioning my level of performance.

Terry was upbeat in the dressing room but we knew as a collective that it was not a good result. The last thing we wanted to do was go into our final group game against Holland having to get something out of it, with the pressure ramped up. We had wanted to alleviate the pressure going into that game. You want your work to be done. But the draw against the Swiss meant that was certainly not going to be the case. Whatever happened in our next game against Scotland, we were going to need something in the last match against Holland. By not winning that first one, you keep yourself under pressure for the next two.

And I was experienced enough to know that, as far as my own situation went, every mistake puts your position in jeopardy for the next game. I had done some good things in the match, too, but I felt I had cost my team three points and now I knew that my position in the side would be up for grabs.

6

WE WOULD LIKE TO APOLOGISE TO MR GASCOIGNE

THE RESULT AGAINST Switzerland made our nerves worse in the run-up to the second group game, against Scotland. The pressure had not decreased. It had been heightened. We hadn't played well and now we had everything to prove against a team that we knew would love nothing more than to beat us at our own tournament, in front of our own crowd, at the home of English football.

In club football, I suppose the nearest equivalent would be Liverpool playing Manchester United in the Champions League final. The fear of losing would be almost unbearable – almost greater than the thought of winning. Knowing that your bitterest opponents would hold bragging rights over you for the rest of time, with very little chance of ever putting it right, would be too horrible to comprehend. It was the same contemplating the idea we might lose to Scotland in these circumstances. The thought sends a shiver through me even now.

Of course, there was an awful lot to win for us, too. But sometimes the mind thinks more of what there is to lose before an occasion like that. I couldn't think of much worse than losing to the Scots and effectively being knocked out of the tournament by them. We knew how much the country had been anticipating Euro 96, and for it to be ended by the Scots before it had really begun did not bear thinking about.

We had been down that road before. Almost, anyway. Scotland beat us 3–2 at Wembley in 1967 with a team featuring Denis Law, Billy Bremner and Jim Baxter and called themselves world champions because of it. We had never lived that down. If they had knocked us out of Euro 96, it would have been even worse.

A lot of the England players were on tenterhooks before the game. The Switzerland performance had made everyone edgy. Gazza was apparently so keyed up the night before the game that he went to see Terry Venables in his room to seek reassurances that he was playing. By his standards, Gazza had had a quiet game against Switzerland and he was desperate for the chance to atone against Scotland.

Terry made him sweat for a little while and then decided that if he didn't put Gazza out of his misery, he would probably not sleep a wink. He told Gazza he was in. Terry had stood by him through all the fallout from the Dentist's Chair and the damage to the plane on the way home. He was not about to abandon him now.

I was still worried about my own place. I hadn't exactly had one of my better games against Switzerland. If you cost your team a penalty, you are always particularly hard on yourself. And then being turned over in the corner by Türkyilmaz and the opposition nearly scoring didn't help either.

In any game, you only do one or two really good things if you're lucky and one or two really bad things if you are really unlucky. You hardly ever have a complete nightmare, certainly a player of my drive. All you are trying to do is get through games without making mistakes. If I played the best I possibly could, I always told myself I would be the best player on the pitch. That included England as well, even though I was on the pitch with some incredibly talented players who had far more ability than me. But that was still my attitude.

Equally, I wouldn't brush off my own mistakes. It would hurt. If you get done once and it leads to a goal, that is hard enough. If you get done a few times, the chances are you won't last long in the team. I thought it might be touch-and-go as to whether I survived in the starting XI for the Scotland match.

A tournament accelerates the evolution of the team. I went into Euro 96 as the oldest player in the squad and so I knew I was on dodgy ground from the start. Quite often, the first person to go out of the team is the senior citizen. And I always had it in my mind that Terry had made that phone call to me, offering me a way out, a couple of years before. I had no illusions that I was indispensable.

England against Scotland is a massive game. It always has been. It is essentially a local derby of international magnitude. Throw in the mix that this was an absolutely pivotal match, the second game of the group, and it doesn't get much better than that. Or much worse if you come out on the wrong side of it.

The stakes were raised by the fact that we hadn't played the Scots for seven years. The Home Internationals had been discontinued in

1984, so the days of us playing each other every year had long gone. I'd played in the last one, a 2–0 win at Hampden in May 1989 when Chris Waddle and Steve Bull had scored our goals. Gazza and I were the only survivors from that day in our team.

The game meant a lot to me as an Englishman. In terms of rivalry, it was Germany and Scotland out in front when you were an England player. I knew a lot of the players in the Scotland line-up, but to say any of them were my friends would have been a stretch. I certainly didn't have any Scottish friends on that particular day.

I had plenty of memories of what it was like to be an England fan at Wembley when Scotland had played there in the past. It always amazed me that England fans were so outnumbered. The Scots descended on the stadium and turned it into an invasion of London. The Tartan Army and all that stuff. It was like an England away game. I knew that this time it would be different.

In the past, the Scots would colonise London for the day. And the night. They'd be dancing in the fountains in Trafalgar Square. And I've seen England–Scotland games at Wembley where the England fans were penned in the lower enclosures and the Scotland fans were surrounding them. This time, because it was a tournament, England supporters would be in the ascendancy.

I did an interview with Ray Stubbs for the BBC the day before the game and I felt the need to bang the drum about how important playing for England was to me and how seriously I took it. We were being hammered so much by the press that a lot of the players felt as if their commitment to the team and to playing for their country was being seriously questioned.

That seems to be a running theme with England. It still is. Do the players care enough? Are we bothered enough? Are we more interested in winning medals with our big, rich clubs than we are in playing for our country? I think it's unfair. Club vs country is an interesting debate and I can see the argument that the Champions League is the pinnacle of the game from a player's point of view in club football. But I still believe that England players are motivated to play for their country as much as any player for any other country. That includes Scotland. Yes, they are desperate to win. But so are we. We know about the emotions that playing for your country can unleash in the supporters and we wanted to be the focal point of those emotions.

The pendulum has swung back towards England in recent years, with Gareth Southgate making big strides in that regard in the build-up to 2018. He brought the joy back to playing for England. And the run his team went on to get to the semi-finals reminded players, if they had forgotten, of how England can reach football supporters in this country in a way that is beyond club allegiances.

That feeling that the players' commitment was being questioned had got worse after the Switzerland game. Terry had allowed any players who wanted to go out for a drink to wind down after the game to do so, and members of the public took pictures of Teddy Sheringham, Jamie Redknapp and Sol Campbell in Faces nightclub in Ilford. The outcry about the attitude of the players redoubled.

It was like a feeding frenzy. The players had been having a quiet drink. They weren't doing anything against the rules. And yet it was being painted as if they didn't care about the bad result against Switzerland and were purely intent on having a good time. Teddy did an interview that week, too, and I could tell he was smarting from the way he had been portrayed.

It is interesting to compare the treatment we got from the press then with the treatment the England team gets now. There have been periods where players have been made into scapegoats, but at the 2018 World Cup, Gareth achieved a much better atmosphere between press and players and it seemed to help everybody. He did have one issue with a line-up being revealed when a photographer took a picture of a piece of paper with some names written on it that was being held by Steve Holland, Gareth's assistant coach, but it turned out it wasn't the line-up for the next game at all. Social media accused the press of trying to undermine the team then. God knows what they would have made of the way it was in 1996.

Back then, Terry was exasperated by it. He called out the team's critics at a press conference. 'They're turning the public against the players, which can turn them against us in the stadium,' he said. 'We would like them to help us win the games which can take us through, but it seems everything is very negative against the players.

'I gave them a couple of days off after the Switzerland game. I'm not going to say to them that you can have a beer if you win but you can't if you lose. That would make me seem like a silly, little boy. We are trying to get them to stick their chests out and play like men, so they have to be treated like men.

'We just don't understand that it's necessary to do what you're doing. There are a few that seem like traitors to us. They're turning the public against the players. If there's an advantage to being at home, we aren't taking advantage of it, are we? The support isn't as strong as we should have. Therefore the advantage, if there was one, is disappearing.'

Momentum can be weird in tournaments. It can move you

forward but it can stack up against you, too, and sometimes if you don't get the start you need, it can feel as if everything is conspiring against you. The feel-bad stories mount up, like damning evidence at a trial.

There was even one after the Switzerland game – Scotland had also drawn the other opening match in the group against Holland – about how we would suffer because of the rules if we finished level on points and goal difference with one of the other sides in our group. It turned out Uefa had decided to use qualifying records for the last three major championships – Euro 92, the 1994 World Cup and Euro 96 – to decide who would qualify for the quarter-finals. Given that we failed to make it to the USA in 1994 and hadn't been involved in qualifying for Euro 96 because we were the tournament host, we were bottom already.

I put all of that out of my mind on the day of the game. The negativity was difficult but it motivated us, too. I had made the starting line-up and I was pumped up before the start. I was standing between Gareth and Gary Neville for the national anthems. When 'God Save the Queen' started up, Gareth was singing it, I was yelling it and Gary was standing there with his head down and his mouth firmly closed. He never sang the anthem. I think he felt it affected his concentration. It was quite a stark contrast.

I was right in the zone. I don't actually have a problem with Scotland in general, of course. In fact, if England aren't involved, I always want Scotland to do well. But on this occasion, when the two sets of players walked past each other and shook hands, I could barely stand to look at the Scotland players. I didn't want to take anything off the intensity I was feeling. I just wanted the game to start and to tear into it. There was an air of unfinished business after the Switzerland game. There was a lot of pent-up football frustration.

It didn't mean I didn't have any respect for the Scotland side. I did. There were some good players in that team. Colin Hendry had won the Premier League title with Blackburn Rovers the previous season. Gary McAllister was a top-line, top-flight player who had also won the title, with Leeds United, and would go on to play for Liverpool. Gordon Durie was a very good, clever centre forward, brilliant in the air and generally under-rated. They had quality all over the pitch and they also knew they had a lot less to lose than us. They had the added motivation of trying to bury us in front of our own fans and spoiling the biggest party we had thrown for a long time.

I started on the left side of a back three alongside Tony Adams and Gary Neville, with Gareth pushed up into a shielding posi-tion in front of us and Incey just ahead of him. The first half was tight and tense. It was the kind of match where there was a lot of effort and plenty of tackles but very little in the way of chances or highlights. It was attritional.

When the half-time whistle went and we began walking towards the tunnel, there were some boos from the England fans. They were frustrated. They could tell we were struggling. Maybe Terry was right and some of the headlines in the news-papers had got into their heads. It felt as though it wouldn't take much more for them to turn on us properly. I didn't even want to think about what the atmosphere would be like if Scotland scored first.

The television analysts got stuck into us at half-time. Jimmy Hill was in the box that day and he wasn't happy. 'Gascoigne doesn't look physically right, he doesn't look emotionally right,' he said. 'Steve McManaman is never happy on the left, Darren Anderton is in a semi-coma . . . England do not look like an international team.' And so on and so on.

I didn't know it then but my active involvement in the match was already over. When we got back to the dressing room, Terry said he was making a change. He was bringing Jamie Redknapp on and taking me off. Gareth was going to drop back into defence to take my place and Jamie would play in midfield. Terry wanted us to get on the ball more and needed to find a way to fit Jamie into the side.

I could see the logic of it but I was disappointed, obviously. When I made my way back out to sit on the bench for the second half, I wondered if that was the last involvement I would have in the tournament. I wondered, in fact, if I had just played my last minutes for England, given my decision to retire when Euro 96 was over.

Tournaments can be brutal like that. You work so hard for so long to play in them and then maybe things don't go your way and you get spat out the other side. I have seen it happen time after time to players. Nobody's immune. Not even someone as great as Bryan Robson, although in his case, it was injury that cursed him. It's still brutal, though. You're taking a fitness test one day and then you're on the plane home the next.

I was thinking more about the game than my own situation, but somewhere in my mind, I knew I had to be realistic. I desperately wanted us to turn things around in the second half but I knew that if we did, that would probably mean I wouldn't feature in the final group game against Holland and I would find it hard to get back in again.

I suppose the most obvious example of that happening to a player was with Jimmy Greaves at the 1966 World Cup. Greaves was one of the greatest goalscorers there has ever been anywhere and, before the World Cup, it was almost unthinkable that he would not be in England's starting line-up.

Then he picked up an injury in the final group game against France and was replaced for the next match by Geoff Hurst. Even though Greaves regained his fitness, he couldn't get back in. Sir Alf Ramsey stuck with Hurst and Hurst scored a hat-trick in the final. Greaves struggled for a long, long time to come to terms with what had happened to him.

That's probably the most extreme example, and I'm well aware that me being left out of an England team and not being able to get back in would not have had quite the same impact as it happening to Jimmy Greaves, but the general point is the same. Every player fears being left on the outside looking in, and as I walked along the Wembley touchline to take my place on the bench for the second half of the Scotland game, all sorts of conflicting emotions were flying around in my head.

It turned out to be probably the most important half of football in the whole tournament for us. It was the half when we finally cast off the nerves that had been haunting us and restricting us. It was the half when the fans finally embraced us. It was a roller-coaster of a half where things went from good to bad and then to sublime.

The atmosphere seemed to have changed immediately at the start of that second half. The crowd was more positive. The noise went up a level. Redknapp was on the ball a lot, McManaman was flying forward, Gazza won a free kick on the edge of the Scotland area and curled his effort just wide of Andy Goram's left-hand post. The tempo was different.

Soon, we were ahead. Redknapp fed the ball to McManaman and he laid it into the path of Neville, who was overlapping on the right. Neville curled over what was pretty much the perfect cross to the back post, where Shearer was running in. He only needed to make firm contact to score. Alan was never going to miss a chance like that. It was in the back of the net and the roof came off the place.

I was pleased for Neville, too. It was a big moment for Gary, a great assist at a crucial moment in a formative moment of his career. He was a young lad then, not as forthright as he is now on the television but not short of confidence. The thing I liked about him was his approach to the rest of the lads when he joined up. He didn't shout his mouth off. He respected the players around him. There is a pecking order when you arrive and you are an idiot if you walk through the door shouting the odds before you have achieved anything. Why would you do that? Gary was wise in how he approached it. You look around and ask yourself who are the good influences. If he looked to his left, he would see Tony Adams and Gareth Southgate. That was a pretty good start. He wasn't a mute but he knew how to listen.

We should have gone further ahead a few minutes later when Teddy made an absolutely brilliant run to lose his marker at a free kick. Gazza swung the kick over from the left, Teddy spun away from his marker and wheeled away to the back post. He met the ball unmarked six yards out, but Goram made a terrific save with his right hand to keep it out.

It felt in those few minutes as if we were going to run away with the game. It felt as if we had taken the brakes off at last and were unlocking all our potential. But then gradually the Scots began to claw their way back into the game. I didn't mention John Collins in the list of their players earlier, but he was probably the most cultured of them all and he began to exert his influence.

Midway through the second half, he got to the byline and curled in a cross to the back post. Durie climbed above Gareth and got in a terrific header. I was right behind it on my position behind the bench and I thought it was in, but somehow Seaman got his left hand to it and clawed it out. It was a great save.

It was similar in some ways to the one he made from Paul Peschisolido when he was playing for Arsenal against Sheffield United in the 2003 FA Cup semi-final at Old Trafford. Similar in that both times he appeared to claw the ball back when it was behind him, when it was almost a physical impossibility to keep it out of the goal.

Against Sheffield United, Dave somehow got his right hand behind the ball and pushed it away. This time, it was his left hand and he almost knocked himself out against the post as he pushed it out. It was a great save and it was also a reprieve. But the danger wasn't over, because now Scotland believed in themselves again and we were reeling.

Scotland were all over us. Ally McCoist came on as a substitute and got the wrong side of Gary Neville as he ran on to a brilliant through ball. Gary tried to get a touch on the ball but missed and

McCoist went down in the box. My heart was in my mouth, but there didn't seem to be any contact and the referee waved play on.

Then it happened. McAllister sprayed a lovely ball out wide to Stuart McCall and he clipped the ball low into the box. Durie was on it in a flash at the near post and got the first touch to it. Just as he did, Tony Adams flew in. Durie was too quick for him, though, and Tony took his legs. It was a clear penalty. This time, the referee pointed to the spot.

It was tense on the England bench. Terry bowed his head. We knew how much was at stake now. The Scots were playing well. If they scored this penalty, the crowd would turn on us and they would become a weapon for the Scots, not for us. It would be hard for us to turn it around. There were only thirteen minutes to go and the Scots would have been confident of rolling us over. The tension of fighting to stay in the tournament would have become almost unbearable for us.

McAllister took the penalty. Apparently the ball moved on the spot as he was running up to take it, but I didn't see that from where I was. He actually struck the ball very well, but Dave guessed the right away and the ball came pretty close to him as he dived to his right. He jutted out his left elbow and the ball smashed against it and ballooned high over the crossbar.

McAllister stood there for a moment with his head in his hands. I knew that feeling. He must have realised the enormity of what had just happened. He was unlucky. We were lucky. We knew that it might prompt another momentum swing. We just didn't realise quite how quickly and spectacularly it was going to happen.

Scotland took the corner and were penalised for a foul in the box. The teams regrouped. Dave punted the kick upfield from our box and Teddy took it down beautifully midway through their half. With his next touch, he laid the ball out to Darren Anderton on the left touchline and Darren helped it on first time and lofted it into the path of Gazza, who was running through the middle.

Gazza ran on to it. Colin Hendry was with him, shadowing him. The ball was bouncing. Gazza took it with his left foot as he ran and flicked it over Hendry. Hendry tried to turn to adjust to the ball's change of direction but he slipped and fell. Gazza watched the ball as it dropped and then smashed it past Goram on the volley.

The stadium erupted. It was in tumult. Gazza ran to the side of the goal, where there were a load of water bottles. He lay on his back and pretended he was in the Dentist's Chair at the China Jump club in Hong Kong. In a flash, Alan and Teddy and Steve McManaman were standing over him. They grabbed the water bottles and started squirting the water into his mouth. It was a brilliant scene.

Dave's save and Gazza's goal were separated by about sixty seconds. They changed everything. All around us on the bench, it was bedlam. All the tension had gone. You couldn't hear yourself think for the noise and the celebrations. People knew that not only had England escaped to live again, but that they had just witnessed one of the best moments ever at the old stadium.

I'm biased, I suppose, because I was there and because I love Gazza and because I knew just how important it was, but in my mind, that is England's greatest ever goal. Alan scored a fantastic team goal in the next match against the Dutch, but I still don't think it topped Gazza's.

The obvious place to start in terms of England's best strikes is

Geoff Hurst's hat-trick goal in the 1966 World Cup final against West Germany. It was late in extra time and he was exhausted, but he still managed that run upfield and the thunderbolt finish. If a goal gets better the bigger the stage it is played upon, then you can't get any bigger than that stage.

It was a wonderful strike, technically perfect as well as incredibly significant. And, of course, it produced that iconic piece of commentary: 'They think it's all over. It is now.' England thought they had won the game until West Germany scored a late equaliser in normal time. Hurst's third goal, still the only hat-trick in a World Cup final, sealed the result.

Then there was John Barnes's goal against Brazil in the Maracanã in 1984. Watching him slaloming his way through the Brazil defence and then sliding the ball into the empty goal with his right foot, it felt like we had a Samba superstar all of our own. It was the kind of goal when you almost had to rub your eyes in disbelief at how good a dribble it was.

Some of the magic of it stemmed from the nature of the opponents. Brazil had not won the World Cup in Spain two years earlier but most people who loved football had fallen in love with their team. That was the team of Zico and Sócrates and Éder and Falcão, and all the memories of their brilliance were still fresh in the mind in 1984.

When Barnes scored that goal, it felt like we were beating them at their own game. It felt like a goal fashioned on the sand of Copacabana or Ipanema. We are always mocked for playing the long-ball game, for relying on muscular football, hoofing it high to a big centre forward, and yet here we were watching one of our own mesmerise Brazil in their famous gold and green. That was a joyous moment.

The only thing that counted against it was that it was a friendly. Brazil were shorn of all their star names from two years before, but it was still scored in the Maracanã, which conjures up images of the beautiful game. There was prestige to it, too. Mark Hateley, who played for Portsmouth at the time, scored the second goal in our 2–0 win that day. Twelve days later, he had been signed by AC Milan.

Michael Owen's goal against Argentina in St-Étienne in 1998 is a decent shout. I can understand why people would pick that as their best England goal. That was a huge game, too, against a bitter opponent. That was a good Argentina team, with players like Gabriel Batistuta and Juan Sebastián Verón and Diego Simeone, and they were expected to beat us.

That goal of Michael's was about youth and hope, really. It was about a kid who had only just burst on to the scene and suddenly he was running at one of the best defences in the world and cutting it to ribbons with his pace and then smashing the ball past the goalkeeper into the top corner.

It felt then as if we had unearthed a superstar in Michael. That goal changed his life, and even if his injuries cut short the length of time he could stay at the very top, he had a top, top career with England and Liverpool and he won the Ballon d'Or in 2001. In fact, he is the only Englishman to win it between 1979 and now, so it wasn't a bad career.

One of the things I love about Michael's goal against Argentina was the confidence and the fearlessness that ran through it. Even right at the end, when he goes past the last defender, his touch takes him a bit wide and the ball runs right into the path of Paul Scholes. Now, Scholes was a fearsome striker of the ball and it was sitting up beautifully for him, but there was no way Michael was going to give way. He had that lovely certainty of youth that he was going to score and he took ownership of that moment. His body language made it clear to Scholes that Michael was going to shoot and from the moment the ball left his boot, there was no way the keeper was getting anywhere near it.

Some people will insist David Beckham's free kick against Greece at Old Trafford in 2001 was the best. It's certainly hard to argue against it being the best free kick. That was an incredibly tense match and it was starting to look as if we had blown our chances of automatic qualification for the 2002 World Cup when we won that free kick in the last minute.

Beckham had been brilliant that day in the midst of a very poor England performance. Sometimes, it felt like he was playing Greece on his own. But he had taken a lot of free kicks in the game and not succeeded with any of them. There were other players who wanted to take that final one because they knew it was the last chance, but Beckham had the will and the confidence to believe that this time he would get it right.

It was a beautiful free kick, the way it flew in a perfect arc from his boot, over a rather half-hearted Greece wall, and then bulged the back of the net at the Stretford End. There was an incredible explosion of noise after that goal because it meant so much. Sure, it wasn't scored at a major tournament, but it meant England had qualified for Japan and South Korea and would not have to go through the lottery of play-offs.

David famously broke a metatarsal in a Champions League game for Manchester United in the build-up to those finals and there was a suspicion that he was not fully fit by the time England flew out to the tournament. But we got to the quarter-finals and it was that free kick that was the gateway to our qualification.

And one last candidate: Bobby Charlton's goal against Mexico in the 1966 World Cup. I didn't see that much of Charlton but I know that an awful lot of what he did was not flashy or for effect and that sometimes, especially now, it's possible to overlook quite how good a player he was.

But have a look at a replay of that goal some time, the way that he feints to go to his left and then goes back to his right because he was so two-footed that the opposition never knew which side he was going to shoot from. And then there is the shot itself, so cleanly hit, travelling like a bullet past the Mexico goalkeeper, low to start with and then rising and rising until it almost bursts the back of the net.

My favourite goal ever, by the way, is still Trevor Sinclair's flying overhead kick for QPR against Barnsley in the FA Cup in 1997, but despite all those other strikes I've just mentioned, my favourite England goal is Gazza's against Scotland. It had everything. It had the technique and it had the moment. It wasn't a friendly or a qualifier. It was a critical game in our first home tournament for thirty years and Gazza's goal won it for us.

I also love it because of what it said about Gazza. He had taken so much criticism in the build-up to the match. The media had said he was finished and that Terry was being self-indulgent by picking him. Jimmy Hill's criticism at half-time was typical of the stick that was being aimed at him. People were lining up to mock him. I think he was about to be substituted when he scored, but I doubt anyone on the England bench would admit to that now.

I think supporters had begun to believe what they were reading, too. They had begun to believe that the magic had gone and that Gazza was incapable of reproducing the skills he had once possessed. They thought he was washed up and that he was a Terry Venables vanity pick.

His goal against Scotland changed all that. It wiped away all the injury struggles and all the doubts that had beset him and it reminded people that he could do things that no other English player could ever do. So I loved that goal not just because of what it did for the country but because of what it did for the man. Gazza lived for football and that goal was like a redemption for him.

A couple of days later, an article in the *Daily Mirror* seemed to sum up the feelings of the nation. It ran under the headline 'Mr Paul Gascoigne: An apology' and it went like this:

> Over the last two weeks the *Daily Mirror* may have created the impression that England soccer star Paul Gascoigne is a fat, drunken, loutish imbecile who should have been kicked out of the team before the start of Euro 96.
>
> It has now come to our attention that he is in fact a football wizard capable of winning the tournament single-handedly.
>
> We would like to apologise therefore to Mr Gascoigne for any distress our earlier reports may have caused him and send the following message from everyone at the *Daily Mirror:*
>
> *Go get 'em, Gazza, you little Geordie genius!*

Things change quickly in football and there was one more example of that before the end of the Scotland game. Jamie Redknapp had had a superb game since replacing me at half-time. He had changed the course of the match, to be honest. He had made the difference. He had calmed the game down, he had got on the ball, he had used it well and effectively.

He had come into the match cold and had grabbed it by the scruff of the neck. He had done more than enough to keep his place for the next group game against Holland. His performance looked like providing one of those moments when a manager hits upon his team's perfect formula midway through a tournament and then sticks with it.

But football can be cruel, too. A couple of minutes after Gazza's goal, with the match won and everybody getting ready to praise Jamie for the difference he had made, he was alone in midfield when he jumped to try to head a long ball out of defence. The ball sailed over his head, but Jamie landed awkwardly on his right foot and his knee seemed to hyper-extend.

It was obvious straight away that he was in trouble. Actually, it turned out that he had injured his ankle, not his knee, but he was taken off on a stretcher and it became evident later that his tournament was over. Jamie had bad luck with injuries through much of his career and this was one of the main examples of fate frowning on him.

In the immediate aftermath of the game, I was too carried away with what had happened to think about the effect Jamie's absence would have on me. I didn't know the extent of his injury, anyway, and whatever had happened to him didn't change the fact that I had not played well and that I had been hooked at half-time.

What I did know was that we only needed a draw in the final group game against the Dutch to be sure of going through. We were no longer under siege. Tension had turned to celebration. The mood had changed completely.

7

FOOTBALL'S COMING HOME

A ND NOW THE party started. Now it felt like Euro 96 was becoming the festival of football we had all hoped it would be. Until then, it seemed to have been dominated by anxiety: about whether the nation could pull it off, whether we would embarrass ourselves as hosts in terms of the organisation and whether we would embarrass ourselves in terms of the football.

Everybody had been worried about what people would think of our stadiums, what people would think of our public transport network, whether we were able to be seen as hospitable hosts or whether our talent for being a bit starchy would come to the fore. All those anxieties were underneath the surface in the country before the tournament started.

I had felt that anxiety among the players and I had certainly felt it among the fans. There was an unwillingness among the supporters to let themselves go and believe that this could really be something to celebrate. They needed some evidence that Euro 96 could be something special, and the result against Scotland and the way Gazza's goal sealed it gave them the first evidence that was happening.

Gazza's goal and the celebration afterwards became the symbol of something. It tapped into the new confidence in English football that had begun to be felt by the formation of the Premier League and its early successes after so many years of hooligan shame. Gazza's goal fed on the idea of new beginnings.

That goal against the Scots was only one goal, but England supporters latched on to it as evidence that the English game need not be one-dimensional and stolid. It could be expansive and exciting and it could thrill with individual skill. It didn't need to be about long-ball and our old-fashioned virtues. It broke us out of our stereotypes.

It helped Terry immeasurably, too. It was a vindication of everything he had been trying to do. Partly that was because the goal epitomised the reasons why he had kept faith with Gazza when so many people were urging him to abandon him and ridiculing him for sticking by a player who everybody was saying was now past it.

Gazza and Terry had become joined in the public mind. Their fates were intertwined. If Gazza failed, then Terry would fail, too. But if Gazza succeeded, if Gazza dazzled, then it would be a great victory for Terry because he had championed Gazza when all around him were cautioning him to cut him loose.

And partly it was because the Scotland result was also achieved by the way Terry had had the courage to change things around at half-time. When José Mourinho arrived in English football, we lionised him for having the boldness to substitute players in the first half if he was aware that his side was being tactically outwitted. He was not afraid of being radical. He was not afraid of humiliating players if he felt tactics warranted it.

That was what Terry did against the Scots. He could see that our formation wasn't working and that we weren't getting on the ball enough. He could see that we were playing into Scotland's hands. He could see that we were playing to their strengths and not to our own. And so he changed it. I was the victim of the change, but it was impossible to argue that it wasn't the right change.

I didn't feel humiliated, by the way. It is the manager's right to make that kind of decision and I respected that right. We didn't play well in that first half against Scotland. And time was starting to run out. If we got a bad break and they went ahead, we would have been in trouble. I didn't want to go off, but I could see why Terry made the move when he did.

Even as we walked off the Wembley pitch after the Scotland game I knew things would be different. The stands were still full. It felt as if hardly anyone had left. Everyone wanted to stay and savour the moment, and the supporters were rocking and swaying in the old stadium.

That was when I first became aware of what an anthem 'Three Lions' was becoming. It was the first time I remember it sending tingles down my spine. If I'm in the car today and it comes on the radio, it still has the same effect. It takes me back twenty-five years in an instant. It was the sound of that tournament. It was the sound of football's new popularity.

A week before the tournament, David Baddiel and Frank Skinner, the comedians who had written the song with the Lightning Seeds, turned up at Burnham Beeches with a tape and played it in the dining room in front of all the lads. Everyone was a bit nonplussed by it at the time. Given my punk roots, I listened to it and thought it was nothing special.

I soon changed my mind. We helped with a video that Baddiel and Skinner put together to go with the song. The video featured a lot of the great moments from England's football history: Nobby Stiles doing his jig after the World Cup victory, that goal from Bobby Charlton in the game against Mexico, Lineker's equaliser against West Germany in the 1990 semi-final, Gordon Banks's save against Brazil in 1970, and Bobby Moore's tackle to dispossess Pelé at the same tournament.

They got some of us to recreate those moments. Steve Stone did Nobby's jig, Teddy Sheringham scored the Charlton goal and did the leap of celebration afterwards, Robbie Fowler re-enacted Lineker's strike and they got me to execute the Bobby Moore tackle, with Pelé substituted for Baddiel. It wasn't long before I was hooked on the song like everyone else.

After the Scotland game, it was amazing when you heard the song in the theatre that is Wembley. The whole crowd was pumping it out game after game. It became an anthem and I think it still encapsulates somehow what the tournament came to mean to England supporters.

It's a nod to nostalgia and what it means to be an England fan. It's about the pain and the joy of football and the hope and the despair. I think that's why it caught on, really, and as the tournament progressed, we used to play it in the coach on the way to and from games.

Sometimes, we listened to highlights from the commentaries by Jonathan Pearce on Capital Radio, too. His excitement and the screaming and yelling when we scored also seemed to capture the mood of the country at the time. When we travelled back to Burnham Beeches from Wembley after that Scotland game, it was the first time I really noticed the red and white flags flying from car windows and plastered in the windows of pubs and houses along the route. The mania that we had all hoped would take hold of the country was starting to be mobilised, but we knew that we had to get something out of the game against Holland to make sure we didn't blow it.

We went into the Dutch game in a positive frame of mind. That was mainly because of the way we had turned things around against Scotland, but we also knew that there were problems in the Holland camp. One of their best players, Edgar Davids, had apparently fallen out with the manager, Guus Hiddink. He had started Holland's opening group match against Scotland but the Dutch were disappointing in a 0–0 draw.

The Dutch had a history of imploding. Internal squabbling had ruined campaigns before. It was reported for a long time that Johan Cruyff had refused to go to the 1978 World Cup because of rows with the Dutch FA, although he later said that he had changed his priorities in life after he had been the victim of a kidnapping attempt.

There were also rumours of racial divisions within the Dutch camp at Euro 96. Before the tournament, there was a famous – or notorious – picture taken of the Dutch squad sitting at a group of tables outdoors having lunch. There were three tables, with seven or eight players on each table. All the black players were sitting at one table. All the white players were sitting at the other two tables.

The Dutch said it was because the chef had cooked some special Surinamese food for the black players and that was why they were all sitting together. I've got no idea what the truth was, but we were aware of all sorts of stories of factions and discontent coming out of the Holland camp. We also knew that they still had some fine players who were capable of causing us problems if they got their act together and put their issues behind them.

It looked as if they might be doing just that when they beat Switzerland 2–0 in their second group game, but Davids was left out of the starting line-up for that match. He came on ten minutes from the end in place of Ronald de Boer, but the damage was already done and the day after the game, he flew home to Holland. The divisions in the camp were right out in the open.

That was our good fortune, I suppose, but we knew there was also a possibility that the departure of Davids would have drawn a line under the problems in the Holland squad and that they would come out all guns blazing against us at Wembley. The fact that they had beaten Switzerland, who we knew were a decent side, certainly suggested that playing them would not be an easy task.

It gradually became apparent in the build-up to the match that the injury to Jamie Redknapp had handed me a reprieve and that I would start the game against Holland. Jamie would have kept his place, but now that he was out, Terry decided to go back to a four-man defence and that meant me starting at left back.

Terry wanted to combat the threat of Jordi Cruyff and Peter Hoekstra, who played wide in the Dutch 3-4-3 system, and that was crucial to him drafting me back in. I knew there would be no more second chances for me. I didn't feel I had done myself justice in the tournament so far, but this was my opportunity to put that right.

Now that I'm old enough and experienced enough to know how a manager thinks, I view myself as very, very fortunate to have stayed in that team. Without the injury to Jamie, there's no doubt I would have been out, and defenders tend to find it an uphill struggle to force their way back in during a tournament. Purely from a personal point of view, I got a lucky break.

Those extra couple of points we had won against Scotland had changed everything for us. You can't overplay what it does when you win a match in the group. You wish you could start every tournament with that same positive mentality, but you have to earn the right to relax into games.

We started well against the Dutch and Alan Shearer had a shot cleared off the line by Richard Witschge. I felt I was doing my job well defensively and when Cruyff broke down the right midway through the first half, I blocked his cross and it went out for a corner. Teddy Sheringham cleared the ball when it was swung in and we broke away.

Steve McManaman charged up the right with it and held it up and held it up until support arrived. Then he laid it into the path of Paul Ince, who took it beautifully and flicked it with his trailing foot. It fooled Danny Blind, who tripped him in the box. Blind was booked and Alan buried the penalty, hitting it hard and low to Edwin van der Sar's right.

The goal was a good example of McManaman's worth to the team. He wasn't always appreciated in his playing days as much as he should have been, but he was a master of the art of transition in football before people really talked about transition. He could transform defence into attack with his pace and his close control. He had great stamina, too.

An individual who can move the ball quickly over long distances from defence into attack is key to a game, especially when you have a player like McManaman who can recognise weaknesses in the opposing team as they are scrambling to organise themselves as they adapt from attack back to defence. The way McManaman set up Ince for that penalty was a classic case of transition being done well.

McManaman was a terrific ball-carrier. He was always viewed as a good player when he was at Liverpool throughout the 1990s, but he suffered a bit from the Spice Boy tag he acquired there with players like Robbie Fowler and Jamie Redknapp. Because they could never quite dethrone Manchester United, they were always accused of having more style than substance.

That wasn't really fair and it was only when Macca moved to Real Madrid in 1999 that he really got the credit he deserved. Macca was only the second England player ever to play for Madrid at that point in their history – Laurie Cunningham was the first – and he won the Champions League at the end of his first season there, scoring a tremendous volley in the final against Valencia, where he was the man of the match.

McManaman travelled well. He was a bit like Gary Lineker had been when he went to Barcelona. Macca was no Little Englander out in Spain. He embraced the local lifestyle, he learned the language, he mixed well with his team-mates and he was loved by the crowd and the media. He did himself proud out there and his reputation grew and grew.

He won a second Champions League title at Madrid in 2002 before he returned to England. I managed him briefly when I took over from Kevin Keegan at Manchester City, but he was past his best by then and he didn't play again after he left City. For a player with such a stellar club record, he only played thirty-seven times for England.

His weakness, I suppose, was that for a very offensive player, he didn't score goals. I rarely saw him get it out of his feet and really smash one. He would rather pass it ten yards than beat someone and unload one, but he was incredibly important to that Liverpool team that he starred in.

Not long after Euro 96, I had a brief spell as caretaker manager at Nottingham Forest and during that spell, we played Liverpool and Middlesbrough. In those two games, there was one individual in each team that I thought was so critical to their side that we had to man-mark him: Juninho at Middlesbrough and McManaman at Liverpool.

At Liverpool, Macca had almost free rein to go wandering wherever he wanted. People who can carry the ball 40 or 50 yards and get your team up the pitch are absolutely vital and Macca was brilliant at that. When I had him at City, he was there with Robbie and the pair of them were in their element.

It was a far cry from the wealth they have at City now, mind you. I came in with no money and I was trying to fiddle around with the budget and get some youngsters in the team with legs. As a bloke, Macca was fine. His attitude was spot on. He's a sensible bloke.

When he was at Liverpool, he fell into that category of the white-suit boy-band brigade and I don't know whether that helped or hindered his career. He had talent and he went to European Cup finals and played for one of the biggest teams in the world. Robbie's not as daft as some people make out, either. He was a decent kid.

I think they both suffered from being part of a Liverpool team that lived in Manchester United's shadow. They were part of Liverpool's thirty years of hurt that has only just come to an end. Because they couldn't break United's stranglehold on the Premier League, people concentrated on their shortcomings instead of their qualities.

After Alan's penalty the Dutch rallied and Dennis Bergkamp guided a header wide when he got above Tony Adams. Incey was booked for a foul on Jordi, which we knew would put him out of the quarter-finals if we got there. Just before half-time, Clarence Seedorf whistled a decent shot just over the crossbar from 25 yards out. We were still in a fight.

The game is remembered now for some of the sparkling football we played, but our second goal, five minutes after half-time, was route one from a set piece. Sheringham was absolutely superb at finding space at corners and when Gazza hit one deep to the back post, Teddy got above his marker and headed it towards the corner of the goal.

It was a good header but I expected Van der Sar to save it. The goalkeeper appeared to be put off by the presence of McManaman darting around in front of him, though, and seemed to think it was going wide. He didn't make a proper attempt to save it and it flew past him and nestled in the corner. There was great elation about the goal, obviously, but there was surprise on the faces of the England players as they celebrated, too.

The goal felt like a gift. It gave us a cushion. It gave us even

Six years after Turin, I was bricking it as I placed the ball on the spot against Spain.

I hit the ball with enough power to beat keeper Andoni Zubizarreta, although he dived the right way.

'Come on, come on!' With all the pent-up emotion, I couldn't stop myself screaming to the crowd.

David Seaman kept out Miguel Ángel Nadal's penalty, sending us into the semi-finals.

Dave was immediately engulfed by his ecstatic team-mates and the England substitutes.

After the Spain game, Gareth Southgate and I introduced the Sex Pistols at Finsbury Park . . . his first gig!

Eleven Lions ready to face Germany at Wembley. *Back row*: Ince, Platt, McManaman, Seaman, Southgate, Shearer. *Front*: Gascoigne, Sheringham, Adams, myself and Anderton.

This crass, disrespectful front page before the semi-final only served to fire up Germany.

My lapse in concentration let in Stefan Kuntz to cancel out Alan Shearer's early breakthrough.

Matthias Sammer, here taking on Paul Gascoigne, became the tournament's most influential player.

Andy Möller was unimpressed by my offer of a helping hand after Paul Ince fouled him.

Gazza cut a forlorn figure after being inches away from scoring a Golden Goal winner.

My penalty wasn't the best, but fortunately for us, keeper Andreas Köpke went the wrong way.

Thomas Hässler's penalty was perfect for power and placement, giving
Dave Seaman no chance.

I knew how Gareth was feeling after
his kick was saved, but that was no
consolation to him.

All of a sudden, Euro 96 was over for me and
for England – and it was such a wretched,
empty feeling.

My England side beat Sweden on penalties to reach the 2009 Uefa Under-21 final, watched by myself and the entire England party.

I went against Fabio Capello's wishes in 2010 to brief David James on penalty-takers.

England finally won a World Cup shoot-out in 2018, against Colombia, to my old team-mate's delight.

more freedom to play. And five minutes later, we scored another of the great goals in England's history, to go with the one Gazza had scored against the Scots. If Gazza's was an example of individual brilliance, this was a team goal, a goal that is remembered for the build-up as much as the finish.

It started with a mistake from the Dutch. Van der Sar collected a long throw from Gary Neville and rolled it to Michael Reiziger. Reiziger tried to break forward and clipped the ball inside to Ronald de Boer, but De Boer let the ball run under his foot and Tony Adams picked up the loose ball. Gazza was alongside him. Tony gave it straight to him.

Gazza moved forward and rolled the ball out to Anderton on the left. Anderton rolled it back to him. Then came the moment that unlocked the Dutch. Gazza quickened the tempo. He played the ball sideways to McManaman and then accelerated forward, looking for the return. Seedorf was marking him but didn't track his run.

McManaman found Gazza expertly with a ball of just the right weight and direction and suddenly the Dutch were stretched out of shape. Aron Winter tried to go with Gazza and tackle him but Gazza shrugged him off and left him on the deck.

Now Gazza was deep inside the Dutch area, cutting in from the left and with options to his right. Blind came to close him down. Gazza thought about trying to dribble past him, but he was too intelligent a player to do that when he saw the other options. Gazza was always aware of everything around him. He saw Teddy Sheringham in space and flicked the ball to him with the outside of his foot.

Teddy was only about ten yards out. He could easily have shot himself. He certainly would have been entitled to shoot. Most people were expecting him to shoot. But as Johan de Kock, a second-half substitute, took a step towards closing Teddy down, Teddy opened his body and helped the ball on towards Alan Shearer. It was a beautiful, deft touch. It was so clever, so well disguised, that it took De Kock totally by surprise. He was so startled by the change of direction, in fact, that he fell over and the ball rolled gently into Alan's path.

Alan ran at it and lashed it towards the top corner. It was a perfect strike. He hit it with a bit of slice and as Van der Sar rushed out to try to meet him, the ball hurtled past him and went like a rocket into the roof of the net. It felt like the perfect team goal. 'You have to say,' Barry Davies said on the commentary at the time, 'that is magnificent.'

There was almost an air of disbelief at Wembley. It seemed like a very un-English goal to score. It was a goal that tipped its cap to that great Carlos Alberto goal in the 1970 World Cup final against Italy. In the final moments of that move, Pelé gets the ball on the edge of the area, just as Teddy got the ball against Holland. Pelé takes a touch and rolls it into the path of Carlos Alberto, just as Teddy had rolled his pass into the path of Alan.

I love that touch of Teddy's. I watch it again and it almost feels like he underhit it. If the defender had read it, he could have cut it out easily. But that's the beauty of it. That's the skill of it. That's the ingenuity of it. Because the defender didn't read it. It went against everything he expected. He was expecting Teddy to shoot, because that's what English players do in that situation.

It was almost like Teddy threw away a national stereotype in that moment. I think that was part of what made that goal so intoxicating. It is one reason why it will always be cited as one of the great England goals. Because it was so un-English. Because it was the kind of goal that England fans think we never score.

It was the kind of goal other supporters would say we could never score. That we didn't have the technical ability to fashion a goal like that. That's why we love it. Because that goal defied all those stereotypes and those attempts to pigeonhole us as limited and lacking imagination. That's why that goal will always be imprinted on our national football psyche.

It was amazing how quickly things had turned for Teddy. It was only ten days earlier that he was being lambasted by the press and the public after his trip to Faces. Before that, he was one of the players singled out after the China Jump club escapade. Now people were finally talking about what a clever, thoughtful, unselfish player he was.

The same was true for Alan. What a transformation in his fortunes. At the start of the tournament, his critics were saying he should be dropped and that Terry was being foolhardy for sticking with him. Now he had four goals in the tournament already and was leading the race to be its top scorer. He, too, was getting the recognition he deserved.

It wasn't long before Teddy got the second goal that his all-round play warranted. He started and finished the move for our fourth goal on that golden evening, flicking on a ball for Alan to run on to. Alan held it up well and laid it back into the path of Anderton. Anderton's low shot took a slight deflection off Blind and was well saved by Van der Sar, but he could only parry it and Teddy rifled home the rebound.

It was always said about Teddy that he was not the quickest player, and maybe that was true. But when Van der Sar parried that shot from Anderton, Teddy got to the rebound faster than defender Winston Bogarde. That was because what Teddy lacked in pace, he more than made up for in his reading of the game and his gift for anticipation. He had the knack of knowing where the ball was going to be.

This felt like fairy-tale stuff now. We were four goals up against the team who had been the pre-tournament favourites and there were still twenty-five minutes to go. Four goals up and cruising against the side that was supposed to be the best team in the competition. Four goals up and feeling like we were getting better with every match that we played. Four goals up and with the crowd fully and ecstatically behind us.

We could have had more. Anderton came within inches of latching on to a cross from Macca and the Dutch didn't know what had hit them. We were playing superbly. The understanding between the players going forward was bound to grab all the headlines, but we had been excellent all over the pitch. Gareth and Tony had been outstanding in the heart of the defence, reading the game brilliantly. I'd had my best game of the tournament so far. I hadn't given Jordi a sniff.

They brought Kluivert on in the closing stages. I'm not sure why he hadn't come on earlier. Maybe he was coming back from injury. But you could tell what a class player he was. He had only been on for six minutes when he ran on to a typically astute pass from Bergkamp and slid the ball through Seaman's legs. I was gutted that we had thrown away our clean sheet.

Part of the reason for that was that I knew how important it would be to keep the opposition out in the closing stages of the tournament. Goals were going to be a lot harder to come by, so that meant we had to be especially tight at the back. Kluivert scoring that goal was the only negative from the evening.

I've talked a lot about favourite goals and favourite moves but I'm a defender and a lot of the time that is how I judge matches and performances. I love good defending and that doesn't always mean a thundering tackle. Of course, there are tackles I admire. I remember one from Micah Richards in a Manchester derby that was a masterpiece of aggression and timing.

My favourite save is an obvious one: Gordon Banks for England against Brazil in the 1970 World Cup, when he pushed Pelé's header over the bar somehow. That save still astonishes me when I watch it now. It seems to defy the laws of physics.

The best tackle I made was for West Ham against Spurs in the quarter-final of the FA Cup in March 2001. We lost 3–2 but there was a tackle in that game where Les Ferdinand was going through for Tottenham and he was just about to unload one and I slid back and flicked the ball with my left foot and got it out.

But picking your favourite pieces of defending is harder than picking the attacking equivalents. Great goals speak for themselves. They're obvious. Sometimes, it's harder to isolate a great moment of defending. There are a few obvious ones like that Moore tackle on Pelé or a fantastic goal-line clearance, but often it's more subtle than that.

It might be a passage of play when you are left isolated and you have to play a mental game with the attackers. You have to be smart. If you are being attacked two on one, the one thing you cannot do is let him pass that ball to his mate because once he gets the pass away, you are finished. You have to sit in a position where you put the onus on him to play it, sow a seed of doubt in his mind.

There was a moment at Stamford Bridge in the match that ended up handing the league title to Liverpool in June of the 2019–20 season when Chelsea's Christian Pulisic was running at Manchester City's Benjamin Mendy. Other defenders were racing back to cover and Mendy just needed to hold Pulisic up for a few seconds to let his team-mates recover their ground. But instead of doing that, Mendy lunged at Pulisic and tried to tackle him. Pulisic was way too quick for him, nicked the ball away from him and was clean through on goal. Pulisic scored and the moment was held up, quite rightly, as an instance when City's defending had let them down.

When that kind of defending is done properly, though, it is spectacular. Virgil van Dijk provided a brilliant example of it in the 2018–19 season when he was playing for Liverpool against Spurs and Moussa Sissoko broke forward with the ball with Son Heung-Min to his right and only Van Dijk between both of them and Liverpool's goalkeeper, Alisson.

Van Dijk backtracked, using his body position to cut off the ball to Son while simultaneously tracking Sissoko's run. Van Dijk's tactic also forced Sissoko to take the ball on to his weaker left foot. Van Dijk didn't panic. He said, 'How are you going to beat me?' He sowed that doubt in Sissoko's mind. And in the end Sissoko had to commit to going alone. He hit the shot with his left foot and it sailed over the crossbar.

There's as much beauty in that, for me, as there is in a great goal. Sometimes, there is as much beauty in destruction as there is in creation. Sometimes football is about stopping the creative players on the opposition side as much as it is about creating chances yourself.

Anyway, I was disappointed we had conceded against the Dutch. I was also disappointed, to a degree, for the Scots. I didn't want them to do well at our expense, but when it was obvious we were going through, I hoped they would, too. They beat the Swiss 1–0 in the final game, with a goal from Ally McCoist, but Kluivert's late goal for Holland against us put them out on the goals-scored rule. That was cruel.

Our performance was hailed straight away as one of the best by an England team down the years. Our detractors would say that we didn't have a particularly high bar to clear in that respect, particularly at major tournaments, where we have cultivated an unfortunate habit of not being able to get past the big teams. This was different.

In the twelve years I played for England, it was the best performance by a country mile. It wasn't just a result we ground out. We played confident, expansive, pass-and-move football and we blew accomplished opponents away. Playing in that game felt like being part of a new dawn for the English game. It sounds naive now, but it felt as if the only way was up.

I guess it must be up there in England's all-time list, too. I can think of plenty of good performances over the years but some of them, like the second-round tie with Argentina in St-Étienne in 1998 or the 1990 World Cup semi-final against West Germany or the 1970 quarter-final defeat against West Germany, have ended in defeat, so it's hard to include them.

England played extremely well against France at Euro 2004

for most of the game but contrived to lose it. When we beat Croatia 4–2 in the third group game, I thought we had a really good chance of winning the tournament. The form Wayne Rooney was in made us look almost unstoppable. If he hadn't got injured in the quarter-final against Portugal, we would have been hard to beat.

There was a game in 1987 that doesn't seem to get much of a mention now when England beat Spain 4–2 in Spain and Gary Lineker got all four goals. It was a friendly, sure, but any time you score four goals at the Bernabéu, it's a pretty good effort. I've seen some people shout up our 3–2 win over Spain in Seville in the Nations League in 2018, too.

Beating Croatia 4–1 in Zagreb in a World Cup qualifier in 2008, when Theo Walcott became the youngest player ever to score a hat-trick for England, was a landmark result, too, because Croatia were a good side then and we were coming off the back of not qualifying for the 2008 Euros.

And there is an obvious case to be made for the 5–1 victory over Germany in Munich in 2001 when Michael Owen scored a hat-trick and we humiliated our most bitter rivals. That was an amazing occasion for any England football fan, because it turned recent history on its head and confounded our own expectations.

I remember hearing stories of the England journalist Steve Howard lighting up a cigar in the press box at the Olympic Stadium in Munich when we scored our fourth goal. And when we scored the fifth one, he lit up another and smoked them both at the same time from opposite corners of his mouth.

I loved seeing pictures of the scoreboard from that night in Munich. The '1 : 5' looked beautifully stark in those giant numbers. It was one of the great scoreboards, a bit like when England scored 517–1 in the first Ashes Test in Brisbane in 2010. Because of the way the Aussies score, it read '1/517'. It was beautiful whichever way you looked at it.

That was undoubtedly a great win over Germany in Munich, but the thing about it that always sticks in my throat is that even though we battered Germany in that match, they still qualified for the 2002 World Cup through the play-offs. And when they got to the tournament, they reached the final, while we got knocked out in the quarters.

I think you have to take into account the importance of the game when you are analysing a performance. In that respect, perhaps it's hard to get past beating West Germany in the 1966 World Cup final. But then my understanding of that match is that it was not necessarily a scintillating performance, just a fantastic triumph.

In the same way, Liverpool's victory over Spurs in the 2019 Champions League final was a momentous triumph, but it didn't come close to matching the performance they had produced when defeating Barcelona 4–0 in the second leg of the semi-finals.

So I think our victory over the Dutch at Euro 96 is hard to beat. I'm biased because I was involved, but it had the added ingredients of coming at a major tournament and being played in front of our own fans. It meant more because of that. It meant more because it helped to define that summer and it gave England fans who were there and who were watching at home memories that will live with them for ever.

The victory over Scotland had lifted the tension that was gripping England fans, but the manner of the victory over Holland ignited the whole tournament and turned the atmosphere in the country right up to fever pitch. Gazza's goal against Scotland will be the thing remembered by populists, but the victory over Holland will be the thing remembered by purists.

The win over the Netherlands sent confidence coursing through us all. They were the pre-tournament favourites, remember, and we had just demolished them. You can say whatever you want about Davids and splits in the camp, but they were still a good side with good players and we had outclassed them. We were on a roll and we knew then that we would be hard to stop.

When Alan finished off that brilliant team move, I got as carried away as everyone else. With the adrenaline running through me, I was telling myself we had a real chance of winning this tournament. I thought we could go all the way. It was going to take a team and a half to stop us, especially on home soil.

I knew that if you disregarded penalty shoot-outs, I had only been on the losing side for England on five occasions in sixty-eight games. After we beat Holland I knew that, statistically, things were loaded in my favour, particularly at Wembley, in front of our own fans. When you are part of a performance of that magnitude, you think, 'I could be in the money here.'

I looked around the pitch. There was leadership running right through that team and quality players in good form: McManaman, Ince and Shearer. Gazza wasn't in his pomp any more but he was showing great form too, while David Seaman was the best keeper in the world at the time. So many things coming together. There was the average age of the team, too. Most were 27 or 28. I thought we had every chance.

We had struggled to find form before the tournament and even though we didn't start well against Switzerland, we improved as the Scotland game went on and then everything clicked against the Dutch. Most importantly, the fans believed in us. We're a fan-based sport and to send the fans home as happy as they were on that day takes some doing. Holland was the we-can-win-it game.

On the coach back to Burnham Beeches that night, we were buoyant. We knew we had topped the group. We appreciated the magnitude of the performance we had just produced. The statement it sent out to the rest of the teams was something we felt would help us. But it also told us we were getting better with every game.

8

WHAT'S THE WORST
THAT CAN HAPPEN?

WHEN I WAS at Nottingham Forest, I practised penalties every Friday after training. Even when I wasn't the club's designated penalty-taker, I practised. I suppose the thought of their importance had been seared on my mind, the thought of the highs they could bring the winning team in a shoot-out and the lows they could inflict on the losers.

I developed a practice routine with the Forest goalkeeper, Mark Crossley. I took ten penalties at him. For five of them, I told him where I was going to hit them. For the other five, he had to guess. I wanted to mix it up a bit. I wanted to make it more of a challenge. I knew that you tighten up mentally in front of a crowd, so I wanted to do something to make it harder to score when that pressure wasn't there.

Even when you tell the keeper which way you are going, I found that if you hit the ball hard and true and accurately, it is very difficult for him to stop. My favourite penalty was the whip across my body with my left foot that takes the ball away from a goalkeeper's left hand as he dives. It was easier to generate power with that particular penalty.

If you open your body up and go for the opposite corner, you may get the same accuracy as with the whip across the body but you lose some of the power because you are side-footing the ball. That is where some of the psychological side of it comes into play. You might be willing to sacrifice a bit of power if you have convinced yourself the keeper is going to go the other way.

There wasn't really the option to do that kind of practice when I was on England duty. Not in 1990 and not in 1996, either. I'm not saying it should have been viewed as a priority. Coaching you to win the game before it gets to penalties has to be the priority. But the prospect of a penalty shoot-out was still just an afterthought for the England squad at Euro 96.

Practising penalties was done very much on an ad hoc basis after training at Bisham Abbey during the Euros. If you wanted to take a couple, you took a couple. If you didn't want to bother, you didn't have to. There were five or six of us who wanted to practise, so the option wasn't really there to do serious work on technique.

There was always a queue of us lining up to take penalties against David Seaman and if he had done a decent training session already, he wasn't really in the mood to hang around for another hour or so. So we'd take one or two penalties each and then call it a day. I tried to replicate the conditions I might be taking a kick in, tried to imagine the nerves that would be bouncing around and the tension in the stadium, but it's difficult.

When we qualified for the quarter-finals of Euro 96, I did start to think about penalties more. I knew they were a possibility now we were in the knock-out stages and I knew that they could define a player's career, or at least that people would try to make them define a player's career. Mentally, I wanted to make sure I was ready if it came to that. I wanted to take one. I knew that. There was no question in my mind about it.

Spain had made it through to the quarter-finals by the skin of their teeth, finishing second to France in a group that also included Bulgaria and Romania and sneaking through courtesy of an eighty-fourth-minute winner by Guillermo Amor against the Romanians. After the way we had beaten Holland, maybe people were expecting us to breeze past them into the semi-finals.

They were a good side but they were not in the same class as the great Spanish teams that have dominated European football for much of the 21st century. Fernando Hierro was probably their best player, a giant in any era, and they had Sergi at left back and Miguel Ángel Nadal in midfield, but they did not really have great strength in depth.

Spain were up there with us as the great underachievers of world football at that time. In fact, they were probably ahead of us. This was a time when players like Xavi and Andrés Iniesta were still a few years away from making it into the national team. Spain emerged as a real force in the world game again in the middle of the next decade. Few thought they would be contenders at Euro 96.

The build-up to the game was relatively uneventful. That tends to happen when you are on a high. No one is looking for bad stories any more. They might even turn a blind eye if a player is seen at a nightclub. The appetite for negativity falls away, the newspapers only want to print nice stories and suddenly everything is rosy in the garden.

There was one bit of fun and games. Inevitably, it involved Gazza. He, Dave Seaman and our reserve keeper, Ian Walker, went on a fishing trip to a lake near Maidenhead. Terry Venables liked it when Gazza went fishing. He thought it was one of the very few things that could keep him out of trouble. He thought it calmed him down a bit, if such a thing were possible.

They were out on a boat in the middle of this lake when they spotted a photographer taking pictures of them from the shore with a long lens. Gazza was outraged. They phoned the gate-house and told the guy to shut the gates and started rowing to the shore so they could apprehend this photographer. He realised what was happening and scarpered back to his car to try to make his getaway.

The lads caught up with him at the gate and Gazza said he had to hand over the film from his camera. The guy wound down his window to talk to Gazza but refused to hand over the film. He said the pictures were worth too much for him to do that. So Gazza reached into the car and took his mobile phone and then started to let his tyres down.

Gazza and the others said the bloke panicked at that point and just smashed his way out through the barrier and drove off. The lads dialled the last number he had rung on his mobile and said it went straight through to Piers Morgan, who was then the editor of the *Daily Mirror*. The story appeared in the paper the day before the game, under the headline 'Gazza's Armada; He sets sail for Spanish battle with Able Seaman and Walker the Plank'.

*　　*　　*

We felt confident when we walked out at Wembley. Incey was missing through suspension but David Platt had come in to replace him and we lined up as a 4-4-2, with me at left back and Gareth and Tony in the centre. Everyone expected us to come flying out of the blocks, but fairly soon it became evident that this was going to be an entirely different story from the Holland game.

Tournament football is strange like that. After a low, there can be a high. And after a high, there can be a low. Experience teaches you to accept that not everything will go your way and that you are not going to play fluent football in every match. When you don't play well, you have to ride it and just make sure you get through.

Spain came out hard. Abelardo was booked in the opening minutes for scything through the back of Alan Shearer. It wasn't even a dangerous situation. It felt like he did it just to make a statement. At that time Spain had an unwanted record of going out in quarter-finals and they were determined that it shouldn't happen again. They were up for it.

Alan had a good chance early on but Andoni Zubizarreta made a really good right-handed save to push it around the post. Gazza played the corner short to me on the edge of the box, but I hit it so high over the bar that Barry Davies, on the BBC commentary, made some quip about how I wouldn't even get three points for that.

We got a little bit of a wake-up call when Gazza was caught on the ball in our own half and Javier Manjarín fed the ball through to Kiko. Seaman rushed out to narrow the angle but Kiko slid it past him and into the corner of the net before the referee ruled it out for offside. It wasn't the last time we were to be saved by the linesman's flag that afternoon.

The second time, we got lucky. There were twelve minutes to go until half-time when they played the ball through us in midfield. Manjarín got a fortunate ricochet and as I went to close him down on the edge of the area, he slipped the ball forward to Hierro. Hierro tried to shoot but he made a hash of it and ended up hitting a mistimed toe poke. Our defence moved up but the ball went straight to Julio Salinas. Salinas controlled it with one touch and then clipped it past Seaman into the back of the net. I saw that Tony's arm was up in the air, appealing for offside, and then I saw the linesman's flag go up. I breathed a sigh of relief. Replays showed Salinas was onside. We had definitely had a reprieve.

We used up one more life before the interval. We had an attacking free kick deep in their half and Gazza tried to play an exchange of passes with Steve McManaman. Gazza lost the ball to Salinas and he lobbed a ball over the top of our defence that left Manjarín clear in a lot of space. Seaman came running out to meet him and if Manjarín had kept a cool head, we would have been a goal behind. But Manjarín seemed surprised to see Dave so far out of his goal. He hesitated and then he tried to knock the ball one side of Dave and run around the other.

It didn't work. Dave saw it coming and managed to block the ball and I got back to clear it to safety. We were reeling. After the exultation of the Holland game, it felt as if Wembley was in shock.

There was a bit of 'after the Lord Mayor's show' about our performance. Maybe some complacency had crept in. The form we were in, we thought we were going to roll them over, but the level of our performance fell off a cliff compared to what had happened against the Dutch.

Gary Neville was booked for a tackle on Sergi, who had been causing us all sorts of problems down our right, and that meant he would miss the semi-final if we got there. We were starting to feel besieged. The problems were mounting up. Spain were getting more and more encouraged by the incursions they were making into our confidence.

Alfonso caused us a few problems at the start of the second half, too, and there was one moment when he fell under a challenge from Gazza in the area that caused a few hearts in the stadium to flutter. Fortunately the referee spotted that it was a dive and showed Alfonso a yellow card. We seemed to play a bit better after that and clawed our way back into the game.

Teddy missed an awkward chance after Darren Anderton nodded the ball over the Spain defence for him and Alan went close to getting on the end of a cross from McManaman. Darren smashed a shot across goal from the left a few minutes later, too. We were finally giving them something to think about. Our confidence was coming back.

Our best chance came soon after that. Tony made a superb challenge to thwart a chance for them in our box and we broke upfield. Gazza cut in from the left and drifted a ball over to the back post, where Alan was running in at full pelt. Alan stretched to reach it and it seemed that he only had to touch it to score. He got to it but couldn't control it and somehow it came off his right boot and over the crossbar.

Alan was flying by this point. His confidence was sky-high. He didn't know it yet but he was heading for illustrious company. The list of players who had won the Golden Boot at European

Championships was a who's who of the greats of the game, as you might expect. Gerd Müller had won it in 1972, Michel Platini in 1984 and Marco van Basten in 1988. Alan was at the top of the charts at this tournament, but he couldn't quite break the deadlock against Spain.

We had one more let-off before the end of normal time when Hierro wriggled through our defence on the edge of the box and slipped a ball through to Kiko. Kiko got the ball out of his feet and tried to slide the ball past Seaman, but Gareth came flying in with a brilliant block to clear the danger and that sent the match into extra time.

I started to think about penalties in earnest at that point. I knew that players are tired in extra time and that opportunities are hard to come by. I'd taken the fourth penalty in Turin, but I'd decided I wanted to take the third one this time. I don't know why: superstition, mainly. I wore the number 3 on my shirt so I wanted the third penalty. I didn't think anyone was going to be fighting me for it. It wasn't as if there was any defined order.

We started extra time well enough. It was Golden Goal back then – if anybody scored in extra time, they were the winners immediately – so the cost of making a mistake was even greater than normal and it tended to mean there was even less chance of teams putting it all on the line to try and get a winner in case they left themselves exposed at the back.

Gazza had half a chance when he tried to chip Zubizarreta in the first half of extra time, but the keeper clawed it away. Steve Stone had come on as a substitute and he had an appeal for a penalty turned down. We didn't make too much of it at the time but when I look back at it, he got to the ball first and the defender didn't get anywhere near it when he took him down. The referee waved play on.

We were grateful for one more superb saving tackle before the end, this time from Tony Adams, and then the final whistle went. I didn't feel worried about the prospect of penalties. Actually, I felt energised by it. I went round all our players pointing to my head, telling them we had to concentrate. It was all in our minds now as well as in our technique from the spot. We had to keep our nerve.

We hadn't done a lot of preparation. We'd lined up to whack a few penalties at Dave at Bisham Abbey. That was it. Nobody had shown me any film of Zubizarreta. Nobody had told me anything about his penalty-saving technique or even if he had a penalty-saving technique. In those days, there was no analysis. You just got on with it.

I spoke to David Seaman about it recently and he said he hadn't done any preparation on the opposition. He didn't do any research about which way their players might strike the ball. I don't know whether he wasn't fussed about it or whether it just wasn't done in those days. I suspect it was the latter. Times change.

In today's climate, with the manpower that club sides in particular devote to statistics and analysis, it seems almost slap-dash and amateurish, but that is how it was. 'Marginal gains' hadn't become a thing by 1996. That culture didn't exist, at least not in English football.

Perhaps it depends on the mentality of the manager. If there is a lunatic like me in charge, with my history, it is taken very seriously. But if you are a manager who has never suffered a penalty-shoot-out defeat, you might not place much importance on it until your team are actually walking up to take their penalties – and then you suddenly realise you ought to have done a bit more preparation.

For a long time, it was regarded as something of a novelty if a goalkeeper had done homework on penalty-takers. He was almost considered a freak, a geek, a curiosity. Now, you'd expect it, although it tickles me when some commentators find it amusing that goalkeepers have codes written down for which way a penalty-taker might go in a shoot-out. There's nothing amusing about it. It's called doing your job.

I didn't know it at the time, but Spain were in exactly the same situation as us. Their manager, Javier Clemente, later said that he had not prepared a list of penalty-takers. He was old-school, too. Perhaps everyone was old-school. 'For me,' he said, 'all eleven players on the pitch are capable of taking a penalty. Against England, I approached the first player I had in mind, but he said no. I went to the second and he was happy to take one, but the third also said no. What can you do in these moments? Nothing.'

A lot of managers thought like that at the time. Even when we went to the World Cup in 2010 and I was part of Fabio Capello's backroom team, before our first knock-out game, against Germany in Bloemfontein, Fabio didn't want to give our goalkeeper, David James, any information about who the Germany penalty-takers would be if the match went to a shoot-out.

Jamo wanted the information, but Fabio didn't want to give it to him. Fabio's mentality was that he didn't want to practise penalties. He didn't even want to think about penalties, and he didn't want the players to think about penalties. He thought they would be distracted if they thought like that: they'd be thinking about extra time rather than winning the game.

I had to go behind Fabio's back and give Jamo all the information on the German penalty-takers. I would have had that on the bench with me as well and if it did go to penalties, I would have supplied him with the names of the takers and the directions they take the penalties. Jamo was very thorough in what he wanted. It wasn't ideal, not being straight with Fabio about that, but I thought it was worth it to make sure David was happy and had what he needed.

There was nobody giving that kind of information to Dave Seaman before the Spain shoot-out and, as he said, he didn't feel he needed it. Would he have taken it if somebody had offered it to him, though? Would he have welcomed knowledge about where a taker likes to put his penalties? I'm guessing that he would.

My first thought when the final whistle went at the end of extra time was that I needed to get to Terry to tell him I wanted to take a penalty. It was on my mind because of the history I had. I think I probably knew that because of that history, if I kept quiet, Terry would assume I didn't want to take one of the kicks. Maybe he'd assume I never wanted to take a penalty again in my life.

So I went straight up to him. I told him I wanted to take a penalty. I told him I wanted to take the third penalty.

'Are you sure?' he said.

I told him I had never been more sure of anything. I'd like to say it was because I was thirsting for redemption after what happened in Turin and that I had been waiting for this moment for six long years, that I had been dreaming about it and now my moment had come. But that would not be true. The truth is that none of that had occurred to me.

Let's be honest: after Turin, what were the chances of me taking a critical penalty for England in the finals of a major tournament again? Pretty low, I'd say. I probably wouldn't even have been at Euro 96 if it hadn't been for the injury to Graeme Le Saux. If my move to Japan had worked out, I wouldn't have been at Euro 96, either. If Jamie Redknapp hadn't been injured against Scotland, I might not have played against Spain.

So, no, I hadn't spent every waking hour thinking about having the chance to atone for Turin. I hadn't tortured myself with the question 'When will I next take a penalty at a major tournament?' because I knew the most likely answer to that question was 'Never'. And because I'm a logical kind of bloke, I always left it at that.

I'd put it to bed. Or I thought I had. It happened: I missed, we went out at the semi-final stage, we thought we played well and that was the end of it. But now there was another shoot-out and I wanted to be part of it. I *needed* to be part of it. Not because of personal redemption, but because I honestly believed it would help give us the best chance of going through.

It was never a consideration in my mind to hide and let someone else take the responsibility. I couldn't let Tony Adams or Paul Ince go and take a penalty, or Dave Seaman. It wouldn't have been fair to them. I was a regular penalty-taker for my club. Sure, I'd had one bad experience on a big stage, but I knew how to take a penalty.

I practised penalties. I had thought about penalties. I knew what it was like taking a penalty under pressure. The other players I have just mentioned didn't have that experience, so why would I force them to take one by hanging back? I wouldn't have been able to live with myself if I had not volunteered to take a penalty. It was as simple as that.

It was inconceivable, to be honest with you. I knew it was important, but I could put it in perspective. I have always been the sort to think, 'What's the worst that can happen?' I'm able to compartmentalise things. I understand that it's a high-pressure penalty, but what's the worst that can happen? I miss a penalty again?

Nowadays, I get invited to schools to talk to kids about inspiring others. I tell them that it doesn't matter if you fail; it matters if you don't try. That is the key point here. The real issue is this: if I had just stood there on that halfway line while we lost in a penalty shoot-out against Spain, I would have struggled to live with myself, because I would have known in my heart of hearts that I had shrunk away from a challenge.

So I'm glad I got to Terry. I don't know what plans he had if I hadn't. A couple of the other takers picked themselves, of course. Alan was our penalty-taker. He would go first. Platty would take the second. I would take the third. Teddy had been substituted by then, so he was out of the picture, but Robbie Fowler was on and Gazza was there, too. Once Terry had got over the shock of me putting my hand up, he was probably just happy he had a willing participant.

Alan took the first penalty, and it was a beauty. He hit it hard and high to Zubizarreta's right, and even though the goalkeeper guessed the right way, he never looked remotely like stopping it. Alan celebrated in his traditional way, raising his right hand in the air. We were on the board.

Hierro took the first for Spain. The din of boos and jeers from the crowd was deafening. It took some guts for those Spanish players to step up. Hierro absolutely smashed his penalty, but it was a fraction too high. It beat Dave, but it crashed against the crossbar and ballooned away. Hierro looked distraught.

Platty was next up for us. He went the other way to Alan. He side-footed his shot to Zubizarreta's left. The goalkeeper guessed the correct way again but once again he could not reach the ball. Platty hit it high and it was still rising by the time it hit the back of the net. A bit lower and maybe Zubizarreta would have got it, but he had no chance.

Spain's second taker was Amor. He was under even more pressure, given that Hierro had missed the first one, but he scored with aplomb. He hesitated deliberately during his run-up and rooted Seaman to the spot before clipping his shot low into the bottom left-hand corner, just inside the post. It was a superb penalty.

Now it was my turn. 'A brave man steps forward to take England's third,' Barry Davies said on the BBC commentary. On ITV, Martin Tyler went all psychoanalytic. 'Stuart Pearce is stepping up to cleanse his soul,' he said. I wasn't there to cleanse my soul. I was there to score a penalty. I was there to put us one kick closer to the semi-finals of a major tournament.

Was it possible to shove all memories of Turin out of my mind? For me, yes. The fans might have thought differently. I accept that. I understand why they would have looked at me walking to the spot and thought that the ghosts of that miss against West Germany must be swirling around my head like restless spirits, but, honestly, it wasn't the case. My head was clear.

I suppose a lot of people had got hooked on football at the 1990 World Cup, so I was familiar to them because of what had happened to me there. They would have lived the same emotions as I did. Sometimes you forget that as a player. The fans have lived it too. They have spent hard-earned money to get to tournaments and travel round, supporting England.

I could feel all that as I placed the ball on the spot. I have never known tension like it. I was bricking it, but the supporters seemed to be in a worse state than I was. The truth was that for me the pressure of the situation was not actually quite the same as it had been in Turin. It was only the third penalty and Spain had missed one already.

And if you are going to take a penalty, you want Dave Seaman in goal for your team in the form he was in, and you want to go up when they are behind, which gives you a break in your mind, because if you do miss there is still all to play for.

I could feel that people were desperate for me to score. I could sense it. They wanted me to score for the team and for themselves. They wanted England to go through. But I think they felt something like sympathy for me, too. They didn't want to contemplate me missing another one. They didn't want to think about what that might do to me. They were thinking, 'Please don't miss again.' They knew that if I scored, we would be in a great position to get to the semi-finals.

In Turin, I had smacked it straight down the middle. That hadn't worked out so well. This time, I'd decided I was going to whip it across my body and hit it as hard as I could down low to Zubizarreta's left. That's my safest penalty. I know I generate power when I hit a ball and you generate more when you hit with a whip than when you side-foot it. My thinking was that if the goalie went the right way, he still had to deal with the power, but if I side-footed it and the goalie went the right way, the power wouldn't beat him. So by doing it this way, I was giving myself two chances of scoring: through placement and power.

I also knew that in a penalty situation a goalkeeper has nothing to lose. I don't think a goalkeeper has ever been blamed for not stopping a penalty in a shoot-out, or very rarely. There's that clip on YouTube of a penalty hitting the bar and the goalkeeper running out to celebrate and the camera focuses on the ball bouncing down off the bar and spinning back towards the goal with the goalkeeper oblivious. Sure, the keeper got blamed for that, but it doesn't happen often.

I placed the ball on the spot and walked five or six yards back. I waited for the referee's whistle, which came quickly. I put my head down and started my run-up. I hit it cleanly. I hit it where I wanted to hit it. I hit it where I'd said in my head I was going to hit it. I registered that Zubizarreta had gone the right way, but then I saw the ball hit the back of the net.

And then it all came out. I stopped for a second and then I turned to the crowd. The crowd was going wild. They were screaming. I started screaming at them: 'Come on, come on!' I was punching the air with my left fist, jutting out my chest, my chin was going a bit. I lost it. I am not an emotional man but in that moment, on that spot of turf, at that stadium where I had gone with my parents as a boy, I became a symbol of England's emotion during that tournament.

I became a symbol, I think, of everything that was pent up inside us. I became a symbol of how desperate we had been for Euro 96 to be a success for the nation. I became a symbol of how much we wanted to emulate the Boys of '66 and end the cycle of those thirty years of hurt. I became a symbol of relief. I became a symbol of hope that we were heading to the semi-finals.

There was something beautiful about that moment, too, in terms of what it says about football supporters and human beings. It is easy to see the worst in people sometimes, but the reaction to me scoring that penalty was essentially about human empathy.

I hadn't actually spent the previous six years searching for a means of redemption. I had used that penalty miss in Turin as a source of motivation in the 1990–91 season and, after that, it had become less important to me anyway. But people had seen how upset I was at the Stadio delle Alpi and I think they feared for the effect it would have on me if I missed another.

As a penalty-taker, you're expected to score. I was one of the few people who regularly took penalties. but I was glorified for doing something that should have been expected of me. The focus is usually on the goalkeeper who saves it or the player who misses it. Eric Dier got the winning penalty against Colombia in 2018, but not everyone remembers that.

Maybe my reaction after I scored justified the concerns of those who feared for me if I missed. That explosion of emotion even took me by surprise a bit. I guess it was a combination of my history, the release of pressure in the stands, the wall of noise that hit me and the fact that the penalty took us a step closer to winning a game we could easily have lost.

As soon as the ball hit the back of the net, the circle was complete. I had kept it all out of mind until then, suppressed it all. But when I saw it go in, I backtracked to 1990. My career, and what I talk about to kids, and some of the things I stand for, were all cemented in that moment.

There was the fact that I had been prepared to stand up and go again, even though people were thinking, 'For goodness' sake.' I don't know what the perception would have been if I had missed. Maybe it would have been 'What the hell were you taking another penalty for?'

Once I had scored, those feelings of completing the circle came flooding in. The reaction afterwards was not pre-planned. It was partly a huge rush of relief and partly to stoke the fans up. You could feel the relief on the terraces as well. It was a real high emotionally and a release together.

If I'd missed, honestly, I don't know what that would have done to me. I'm not very emotional in many ways. Certainly away from football, I'm not. As I've said, the only couple of times that I have cried meaningfully have been when I've been involved in football. So football does mean a great deal to me.

Six years earlier, when I missed in Turin, it made me stronger and a better player – more hard-nosed and more determined. I would have expected it to have the same effect if I had missed again against Spain. The difference would have been that it was potentially my last time in an England shirt. The dynamic of that would have been interesting.

It would also have depended on how the shoot-out finished, obviously. But in that moment, it would have been the lowest I had ever felt in my life. But if we had lost, how do you come back from that? I wouldn't have had much chance of springing back from that, because I was 34 years old at the time.

The fact is, I had a twelve-year playing career with England and I am remembered for two penalties. I'm not sure if that's good or bad. You tell me. I am seen as somebody who gives their all for the country and puts the England team up on a pedestal, but boil it all down, I'm defined as an individual who has taken two penalties.

I think the English football public saw a bit of themselves in me. They saw a Sunday league player who had made good through hard work. We had 75,000 in the stadium that day, and millions around the country watching on television, and they would be saying to themselves, 'You know what, if I missed a penalty, I'd stand up and take one again, too.'

There's a clip on social media of a village cricket match and there's a chap at first slip who drops a fairly simple catch off a spin bowler. His team-mates are distraught. He's distraught. Next ball, the batsman edges a much more difficult chance to the same fielder. It's low, it's fast and he's a biggish guy. But he gets down to it and takes a brilliant catch and everyone is made up for him. That was me at Wembley that day.

Maybe that sums me up a little bit. The disappointment of messing up the first one sharpens your focus brilliantly. More than anyone else who went up to take up a penalty that day, my mentality had been focused on a potential penalty shoot-out and a potential penalty kick because I had dropped one in the slips beforehand.

Of course, the shoot-out wasn't over just because I had scored the third penalty. It was a long way from over. Belsué took the third penalty for Spain and sent Dave the wrong way. He side-footed it to the goalkeeper's left and it nestled in the corner. Suddenly, the crowd was hushed again. Spain were still only one penalty miss behind us.

Gazza was next up for England. If people had been desperate for me to score, I was desperate for him to score. Again, that was partly because I knew it would take us to the very brink of the semi-finals if he beat Zubizarreta. But it was also for Gazza. Euro 96 had been such a positive experience for him. It had bolstered him. I didn't want anything to damage that.

I needn't have worried. Gazza was a brilliant penalty-taker. His technique as a footballer was flawless, so why should he be any different when kicking a ball from the penalty spot? On this occasion, he couldn't have placed his kick any better. He hit it across his body, to the goalkeeper's right. Zubizarreta went to his left, but even if he had guessed correctly, he wouldn't have got to Gazza's kick. It was so expertly placed, it almost kissed the post as it went in.

So we were 4–2 up and Spain had two penalties left. Nadal walked up to the spot knowing that he had to score to keep his country in with a chance. I didn't envy him that. It probably made it worse that he knew his team should already be in the semis on the balance of play from the 120 minutes before penalties. They were staring down the barrel of an injustice. They must also have known they would get torn to pieces at home if they blew it again in another major tournament.

Nadal struck his kick well enough, but it was at a good height for a keeper and Dave guessed the right way. He went to his left and got his hands and his body behind the ball and beat it away.

Within a few seconds, Dave was engulfed by celebrating England players and we were into the last four of Euro 96.

We would have to wait until the next day to know for sure that we would be playing Germany, but that was what we expected. They duly beat Croatia at Old Trafford with goals from Jürgen Klinsmann and Matthias Sammer and I knew I was heading for a reunion with my old friends from Turin.

I had had two things in my mind once the tie went to penalties. The first was that I had to score to help us win. The second was that, if we did go through, it was vitally important for me to go over to the Spanish player who missed the last penalty to console him and commiserate with him.

I had been educated in how to be humble in victory by those two German players who had sat in that room with me in Turin and it was really important for me to set the same sort of example to Nadal. I didn't say much. I shook his hand and said how well he had played and 'unlucky'. Clichés, I suppose, but the important thing at that moment is to show some respect.

Terry came over and congratulated me. He said some nice things about me on the television. He still seemed surprised I'd volunteered for a penalty and even more surprised I'd known which one I wanted to take. I went over and waved to the fans and just before we went down the tunnel, Teddy Sheringham came over and lifted my arm up and put it in the air. He pointed at me and shouted to the supporters, 'He's got some bollocks.'

The next morning, Ray Wilkins came up to me at the team hotel and said much the same thing. That meant a lot to me because I admired Ray as a player and as a bloke. It was nice to get praise and I got a sense I was being talked up in the media and among the public. Looking back, I think it was probably a crossroads in the way I was perceived.

When we got halfway down the Wembley tunnel after the game, there was a staircase that led us up to a room where we did 'flash' interviews and they took me and Dave Seaman up there to talk to the cameras. All we could hear was the whole stadium singing, 'Football's coming home.'

That scene is burned on my memory.

I still felt emotional about what had happened. You can see that if you ever watch any of those post-match interviews. The only way that you really appreciate the magnitude of a penalty shoot-out and the effect it can have on players is if you have walked the walk and missed one and your team have been sent home from a major tournament at the level I had.

I wasn't necessarily surprised that we hadn't realised that at the time. Not many of us had been through it. It was perhaps a bit odd that Terry didn't think it was worth practising for, given that he had been the manager of Barcelona when they lost the European Cup final to Steaua Bucharest in 1986. Barcelona missed their first four penalties that night and it cost Terry the biggest prize in club football.

But the general mindset in professional football still hadn't changed much. It was the mindset that Clemente had revealed before the Euro 96 quarter-final. Some managers just believed that every one of the eleven players should be capable of taking a penalty and scoring it, no matter in which order they were selected, and that it was not worth studying the opposition.

There was a fatalism about it all which seems foreign to us now. I think I was an outlier at the time precisely because I had missed that kick in Turin. I was one of only a handful of players that had happened to and it had changed my attitude to penalties and to how you approached them. The experience against Bucharest obviously hadn't had the same effect on Terry.

People talk about having a psychologist involved, but to me that is largely irrelevant. What is relevant is studying the statistics and making sure your five best penalty-takers are taking the penalties. It sounds simple, doesn't it, but it's amazing how often it is ignored. Even now.

When I was at the FA between 2007 and 2013 as the manager of the England Under-21s, we had brilliant performance analysts like Steve O'Brien and Mike Baker and they did a study that basically looked back at every shoot-out in world football. We had every stat on every player who might be playing against us, which is one of the reasons I know Gareth will leave no stone unturned as the current manager of the senior team.

I recognised the analysts' input when I saw the England goalkeeper Jordan Pickford scoring one of our penalties in the Nations League against Switzerland in the summer of 2019. You pick whoever has the best statistics. It doesn't matter whether it raises eyebrows. They would have logged every penalty in every practice and Pickford would have come out in the top five. So he takes one of the first five penalties. You trust the figures. You trust the data.

For the rest of that weekend I felt like I was floating on air. The country went bananas and on our way back to Burnham Beeches after the game, there were crowds lining the road. 'Thirty years of hurt never stopped me dreaming' was going round and round in our heads as the supporters chanted it. You couldn't go anywhere without hearing it.

My celebration after the penalty became one of the images of the tournament. I get that. It was one of the favourite moments of my career. Put it this way, the only picture to do with my career that I have hanging up in my house is one of me bending down to place the ball on the spot before I walk back to take my run-up.

It's not a picture of the celebration afterwards. In fact, in this one, you can't even see my face. It's just the number on my back and the ball on the spot and the knowledge of everything that comes next and the emotions that will be released both within me and for the supporters watching from the stands. And there's the backstory it tells: Venables's phone call to invite me to retire and the fight I had just to get to Euro 96.

That's why it's the only picture on my walls. Don't get me wrong, I love going into people's houses where there are loads of football memorabilia, but I have never been like that. I loved Kevin Keegan's house – it was like an Aladdin's cave of memorabilia – but I have never wanted that for myself. It reminds me of what's gone and not what's in front of me.

I enjoyed my evening with the lads back at the hotel on Saturday night, but my weekend wasn't quite over. I knew that the Sex Pistols were playing at a gig in Finsbury Park the next day and Terry had given us the day off, so I decided I'd try and swing it. I organised some backstage passes and then approached Terry to ask his permission.

I thought it might be a bit touch-and-go after all the extra-curricular issues we'd had. I didn't actually mention the Sex Pistols when I waylaid him in the lobby. I just said that I'd got tickets for a concert and would he mind if I went. I said I'd be back by 9 p.m. He looked a little unsure. I quickly added that Gareth Southgate would be coming with me. That swung it. Terry knew that if Gareth was going, we wouldn't get into any trouble. He probably thought we were going to see Val Doonican.

I think it was the first gig Gareth had ever been to. We headed over to Finsbury Park with a few members of the FA staff, including Steve Double, the head of press. When we got there, we were asked if we wanted to go and meet the band. I thought we'd have some of that, although I'm not sure Gareth was quite so certain.

They were holed up in a kind of caravan with a few friends and family. They were great. John Lydon is a big Arsenal fan, so they were all over the football and what had happened in the Spain game. Steve Jones is the chatterer among them and we had a good natter.

To top it all off, they asked us if we'd introduce them when it was their turn to come on stage. This was like some sort of utopia for me. So we watched Skunk Anansie and Iggy Pop, who were the support acts, and then we got up on stage, looking a bit like Hinge and Bracket in our official England gear, in front of 30,000 music fans. It wasn't quite the most intimidating thing I'd done that weekend, but it was close.

9

SLIDING DOORS

WHEN I WAS the England Under-21 manager, I went to visit the German Football Federation headquarters in Frankfurt. It was a priority for me. People might call it a fact-finding mission, but it wasn't really facts I was after. I knew most of the facts. I knew all about Germany's successes over the years. I had first-hand experience of some of them.

I was more interested in the mentality than the facts. I wanted to get a glimpse into the psychology of German football and the way they prepare for major tournaments. They are an outstanding football nation, with a consistent record of success for the last half a century. Some people see them as our football enemy, but I just wanted to learn from them.

This was some time around 2008. I walked through the door of the DFB offices with another member of the FA staff and we had only been in reception for a minute when one of their guys came through to meet us. He excused himself straight away and said he had something he wanted to show us. He ran off to get it and came back with the front page of the *Daily Mirror* from Monday, 24 June 1996.

There was a big picture of me on that front page. Me and Gazza, actually. Both of us had been mocked up as wearing British army helmets of the type soldiers were issued with in World War II. Gazza was laughing manically and I was pictured in the moments after I'd scored the penalty against Spain, with that look of unbridled jubilation on my face.

The banner headline on the front page read like this: 'Achtung! Surrender.' Underneath our faces with their crazed expressions was another line in big type. 'For you Fritz,' it said, 'ze Euro 96 Championship is over.' Next to it was a column of writing under the headline '*Mirror* declares football war on Germany'. And underneath the masthead, there was one last attempt at a funny line. 'Pearce in our time,' it said.

I winced when I saw it. It was more than a decade old by then and I had forgotten about that front page. But they hadn't. It brought back bad memories for me. I know it was meant to be funny, but when I saw it on that Monday morning all those years ago, a few days before we played Germany in the Euro 96 semi-finals, I had felt embarrassed. On many different fronts, I hated it.

A headline like that in a national newspaper will do nothing but stoke up the opposition. That was what I felt purely from the football point of view. I knew it would give the Germans an even greater incentive to beat us. In terms of our chances of actually winning the game, it was obviously counterproductive.

But the way I felt about it went deeper than that. I thought it was disgraceful. I felt it more because my face was being used to make some war reference or political point. Decode it how you want. Most of all, it was disrespectful to people who fought in the war. I didn't fight in the war and I wasn't a soldier. I thought it was wrong.

In a small way, I'm a bit of a student of military history. I certainly have a huge amount of respect for every single one of the soldiers who put their lives on the line to fight for their country in the Great War and World War II and in all conflicts. I've visited the battlefields in northern France and some of the graveyards and, like most people, I found it an extremely moving experience.

You don't have to look too hard, either, to realise the horrors that those men faced on a daily basis and the courage they had to display from hour to hour. Those generations were strong generations. They knew what hardship was about. I'm not sure how many of my generation, or the ones who have come after it, would sign up these days – or how many would run for cover.

Sometimes, people talk about me and say, 'I would want him in the trenches with me.' I hear that and I think those people probably don't have the moral courage to go anywhere near a trench. That's not even a criticism of them. I just think we talk about wars and what it took to fight in them too glibly now. We have forgotten the levels of sacrifice it took for men to go into a real battle.

That was the main reason I found that front page embarrassing. I thought it was disrespectful to brave men who had fought in real conflicts. Comparing us, footballers about to play a game against other footballers, people who had comfortable lives and didn't know an awful lot about sacrifice, felt all wrong to me. You can call me humourless if you want. I just didn't think it was right.

I thought it was disrespectful to our opponents, too. We have developed a history of doing that in our country and it has usually rebounded on us. I remember when the draw was made for the group stage of the 2010 World Cup finals and we were put together with Algeria, Slovenia and the USA. One paper made its headline the first letter of each of England, Algeria, Slovenia and Yanks: 'EASY'.

We never learn, do we? We scraped through that group by the skin of our teeth. The headline didn't look so clever then. Next up, of course, was Germany in Bloemfontein and they sent us packing without further ado.

Anyway, we were in the reception area of the DFB headquarters in Frankfurt looking at this picture of me from a dozen years before, with a manic expression on my face, wearing a tin hat, under the headline 'Achtung! Surrender'. Why? Because they had kept a copy of one of the things that inspired them on that day.

There was other stuff that we learned. They told us that every time Germany played another team, they found a particular image or article or cartoon or slogan that would symbolise something about the opponent and inspire their players, in addition to all the tactical work they did and the on-pitch training.

They were a bit coy about what they had used when they last played England, but in the end it emerged that they had a cartoon that summed us up as a football nation for them. The cartoon showed a Germany player standing at the edge of a cliff and a group of England players running at him full tilt. And, at the last minute, the Germany player moves aside and the English players run straight over the cliff.

I thought that was genius. How many times have we done that over the years? How many times have we shot ourselves in the foot or found a way to blow it somehow? In the thirty years since we had won the World Cup, the English had met the Germans – either West or reunited – thirteen times. We had lost nine of those games and won only two. I had never been on the winning side against them.

There are lots of reasons for the success the Germans have had in comparison, but one is that they are so thorough in what they do. When I have been in teams against them, I have never felt outplayed by them and yet when it mattered most, they won. You can call it holding your nerve if you want, but why should they be better at holding their nerve than we are? Maybe because they are better prepared and more professional? Just a thought.

Going into the 1996 semi-final, I believed we had a better chance of beating Germany than in 1990. In 1990, I had felt that everything had to go our way for us to win – we had to have our best day and they had to be below par. We had got very, very close in Turin and played the best we had played in the tournament. But no cigar.

As the Germany game approached, it didn't pay to examine the Germans' record in major competitions over the last two decades too closely. West Germany had won the European Championship in 1972. They won the World Cup in 1974. They were runners-up in the European Championship in 1976. They won the European Championship in 1980.

They were World Cup runners-up in 1982. They were World Cup runners-up in 1986. They won the World Cup in 1990. They were European Championship runners-up in 1992. We go crazy when we manage to reach the semi-finals of a tournament. Semi-finals don't really rate a mention for them. That was the level we were up against. This was their sixth semi-final in seven European Championships.

OK, so maybe the Germany team that we were about to play at Wembley was not one of their great sides, but you would do well to catch the Germans ever having a bad side. They had got to the semis very confidently. They had come top of their group and beaten the Croats in the quarter-finals. And if their players weren't quite as high-profile as in some other years, it was no reflection on their quality.

Yet I still went into the game with greater expectation than I did in 1990. That wasn't just because I felt we had a better chance. Remember that in 1990 we had no idea of the public mood back home and the way the nation had been gripped by what we were doing. We were living in a bubble in our camp and in our hotels, and even if we saw newspapers now and then – and ripped them up – we didn't realise how emotions had been mobilised until we got back to Luton Airport to be met by that sea of people.

This time, it was different. This time, we were at home. And now, whenever we came and went from Burnham Beeches, there were crowds outside in the lanes and there were police shepherding people around and directing traffic. There were people lining the streets when we went to matches and 'Three Lions' was playing everywhere and we were listening to replays of Jonathan Pearce doing those spine-tingling radio commentaries.

This time we knew exactly what the mood of the English public was – because we were living it. We knew how much it meant. We could see the effect that football was having and how the spirit of the team had captured everyone's imagination and how the media were getting behind us and the whole thing was building and building and building.

My penalty against Spain had completed the circle for me in terms of banishing anything that had been buried in my subconscious after Turin. But I still felt I had unfinished business with Germany. My mentality was it was just them standing in our way of picking the trophy up. They were all that stood between us and the end of the thirty years of hurt.

I know you can't get to a final and think you are going to have an easy ride in an international tournament, but the other semi-final was between France and the Czech Republic and, as far as I was concerned, neither of them posed as big a threat to us as Germany. Germany knew how to win. They would find a way. It was as if winning was part of their muscle memory.

If we knocked Germany over, there was no doubt in my mind we would win the tournament. The fans would have picked us up and carried us over the line if we had reached the final. We went into the game knowing that we were a better side than we had been and that we had got better and better as the tournament had gone on. The atmosphere had grown to a crescendo. Everything was coming together. I felt we had every chance.

I don't think there was a mental block about playing them. I didn't have one anyway. Perhaps it has developed more in the years that have elapsed since. The first time I played against them was September 1987, when we lost 3–1 at their place, in Düsseldorf, and I came on as a late substitute. That was the start of a run of five successive defeats to them.

But in major tournaments, I played against them in two games that both went to 120 minutes and only penalties could separate us. That's not a mental block. In fact, I've never really viewed it as them coming out on top. They had a better group of penalty-takers than we had because they were better prepared than we were. And that is probably all I would give them credit for. Head to head in matches, the results might weigh heavily in their favour, but there had actually been very little between us. The semi-final in Euro 96 fell right into that category.

*   *   *

We played with a back three that night, partly because Gary Neville was suspended. Many people had assumed that his brother, Phil, would come in to replace him as a like-for-like swap at right back, but Terry had already proved his flexibility with the formation and he stayed true to that.

So Phil stayed on the bench and we started with a back three that had Tony in the centre with me and Gareth on either side of him. Incey came back in after his suspension and Platty kept his place in midfield. I felt we could dominate the centre of the park with that line-up and squeeze Germany out of the game.

They had some selection problems of their own. Jürgen Klinsmann and Oliver Bierhoff, their leading attackers, were both injured, so they had little choice but to go with Stefan Kuntz, who was almost 34. It would be unfair to call Kuntz a journeyman, because he had won the Bundesliga with Kaiserslautern a few years earlier, but he had never played for what we now consider the powerhouses of the German game, Bayern Munich or Borussia Dortmund.

He had been around. The season before Euro 96, he had played for Besiktas. The season after, he played for Arminia Bielefeld. England fans mainly knew him because they could make fun of his surname. His presence in the Germany side was something that was seen as a hopeful sign for us. He may have been a veteran, he may have been a comedian's punchline, but it was all set up for Kuntz to have the last laugh.

We had optimism and belief coursing through us when the game began and we started beautifully. I swung a cross in from the left in the opening couple of minutes and when it was headed out to the edge of the area, Incey took it down and hit a dipping volley that the Germany goalkeeper, Andreas Köpke, punched over the bar.

Köpke could probably have caught it but German keepers tend to go safety first with those kind of shots and punch. That was our good fortune. Gazza took the corner and drifted it in to the near post. Tony Adams rose to meet it and flicked it on. Shearer, who was being marked by Markus Babbel, gave him the slip and ran on to Tony's flick, unmarked.

He had to stoop slightly to reach it, but for a striker of Alan's quality, it was a simple finish. He got his head to it and guided it over the line. It was his fifth goal in five games at the Euros and all those worries about his goalscoring drought seemed to belong to another world now.

Only three minutes had gone and we were already 1–0 up. I didn't get carried away. I was too much in the moment. But I understood why others might have done. Maybe this was going to be the game when we were simply too good for the Germans. Maybe we had been overestimating them. Maybe they were an ordinary side after all. Maybe it was simple: we were better than them and we were going to prove it.

The atmosphere inside the stadium was intense. I could feel the hope coming from the crowd. And I could feel their fear, too. The fear that comes with being ahead. The fear that comes with being so tantalisingly close to something and wanting to protect it but knowing that there is still a long way to go.

There was a real edge to the match. In Turin, the mood between the players had been one of consistent good sportsmanship.

There was almost a camaraderie between us. That spirit was absent here. There was respect, obviously, but it was fractious between us. Gazza went in hard on Sammer in the early stages. He also made a full-blooded challenge on Stefan Reuter.

Gazza was not on a yellow card for this match as he had been in Turin, so maybe he thought he could tackle with a little more freedom. To the modern eye, some of his challenges look reckless now. Some of his challenges looked reckless at the time as well. That was what had caused his serious knee injury in the first place. Others were a danger to Gazza, but he was a danger to himself, too.

It wasn't just Gazza who was flinging himself around, though. Mehmet Scholl responded to those tackles on his team-mates by leaving his foot in on me in a challenge and I squared up to him. It was not the kind of occasion when anyone was going to duck a challenge.

Germany came back at us. They were too good to lie down, whatever some of our fans might have told themselves after Alan's goal. After a quarter of an hour, they equalised. Reuter carried the ball forward and it was worked to Andy Möller on the edge of our box. There didn't seem to be any danger. We had a good shape, we weren't stretched, we were ready. Or I thought we were.

Möller did well. He was surrounded by defenders but he wriggled away from Gareth and as Gazza came to close him down, he slipped a nice reverse pass into the path of Thomas Helmer. I'm not quite sure what Helmer was doing up there in such an advanced position, but he took one touch with his right foot and then, without looking up, he swivelled and hit the ball across the face of goal with his left foot.

I thought Helmer was offside and I raised my hand when the ball was played through to him by Möller. Gareth did the same. But Helmer wasn't offside. I had been aware of Kuntz to my left as that ball was played to Helmer but then I lost him. Kuntz might have been 33 but he was a clever player. I lost my concentration for a split second and he was gone.

The ball came across towards me but Kuntz had drifted off my shoulder and out of my vision, behind me. I started to move towards the ball but then I realised where Kuntz had gone. He had anticipated the ball faster than me and he was on to it in a flash. He came in on the blind side, got across me and in front of me. He had to stretch to reach it but he made a good connection and drove the ball past Dave Seaman with his right foot. I looked over to the linesman, hoping for a reprieve. None came.

We were level and now I had to make sure I stayed strong. I knew I had been at fault for the goal. There was absolutely no room for any more errors from me. I couldn't let it affect me, except to make me play better. I had to use that mistake as a motivation to make sure it didn't happen again. Everyone in the crowd knew now that this was not going to be a parade. We were in a fight.

Terry later mentioned my mistake at half-time. It wasn't a rollicking. Just a reminder. I knew anyway. I knew I had lost the player. That's international football. When you play the blue-chip sides, their movement is that much more clever and it's a game of concentration and chess. Like I said, it almost strengthens my resolve when something like that happens.

At Euro 96, I gave a penalty away against Switzerland, got turned inside out by one of their forwards, got substituted at half-time against Scotland and was at fault for the Germany goal in the semi-final. I didn't dwell on any of it. I gritted my teeth and tried to concentrate on not making another mistake, because the team would not recover from another mistake.

The game swung one way, then the other. Anderton was playing well. He curled one long cross in from the right that Alan dived to reach. He got his head to it about ten yards from goal, but it was just too far ahead of him to be able to get any direction on it and it flew wide.

Darren and Teddy combined for a version of the Tottenham corner that had become famous, where the corner-taker curls the ball towards the edge of the area and Teddy peels away from the near post to meet it. It nearly worked again now. The ball was just behind Teddy but he hooked his right foot around it and it was arrowing low towards the corner of the goal when it was kicked off the line.

Ten minutes before half-time, Gazza went flying in on Reuter and sent him high into the air. He had got the ball, too, but these days an official would say he was out of control and it would be a yellow or even a red. Back then, he escaped without a booking. Not that I could talk: before the interval, I flattened Sammer when we went up for a high ball together. The Germany players weren't happy with that one.

Three minutes before half-time, we nearly took the lead again. It was Anderton, again, who was the provider. He got to the byline and pulled back a perfect cross into the path of Shearer. Alan tried to guide it across Köpke to the goalkeeper's right and into the bottom corner. It went inches wide of the post. Alan was angry and cursed himself in frustration. He felt he should have scored.

Both teams kept pressing after the break. Incey burst forward from midfield but hit his shot high over the bar from 25 yards out. Sammer came running out to berate Möller for not tracking back properly with Incey. The longer the tournament went on, the more obvious it had become that Sammer was this team's true leader.

Germany forced a good chance ten minutes into the second half. Dieter Eilts made it to the byline on our right and cut a cross back into the centre. Kuntz moved out of the way and it ran beautifully into the path of Helmer, who had made another of those forward forays. He hit it first time with his left foot but it flew just over the bar. He should have scored.

Twenty minutes from the end, Gazza made a surging run from the halfway line and when the ball was nicked away from him by Sammer, it fell to Anderton, who played it straight back into his path. Gazza didn't break his stride and it looked for a second as if he were clean through on goal, but Helmer made a brilliant saving tackle.

Gazza finally got his inevitable booking, for a lunging double-footed tackle on Kuntz twenty minutes from the end. Suddenly, the spectre of Turin came into view for him again. One more rash challenge and he could be off. One more lunge and it could be a red card. One more disciplinary error and he could be facing the prospect of missing a final again.

Things grew even more fractious as the stakes got higher and higher and the prospect of the game going into a Golden Goal period grew. Eleven minutes from the end of normal time, Incey caught Möller with a studs-up challenge as Möller hit a shot from the edge of the area. The referee didn't give a foul, but Möller was hurt and he was rolling around on the floor.

I tried to help him up but he wasn't in the mood for being helped by an Englishman. To be fair, he was obviously still in a fair amount of pain. He took my gesture the wrong way and lashed out at me as he sat up. The referee booked him, which meant he would miss the final. Sammer appeared at that point and started accusing me of getting Möller booked. We had a full and frank exchange of views, which he concluded by wagging his finger at me in the manner of a schoolteacher.

I felt for Möller. Not too much, especially not in the moment, but when the game was over, I felt for him. It is strange, though, how something like that can affect different people. When Gazza got that yellow card in Turin, the enormity of what had happened overwhelmed him. He didn't go to pieces, exactly, but it affected him deeply and obviously, to the point where it was obvious it would not be a good idea for him to take a penalty in the shoot-out.

For other people, it seems to reinforce them with steel. When Roy Keane got booked in the same stadium where Gazza had got that yellow card, playing for Manchester United in the 1999 Champions League semi-final second leg against Juventus, he knew that he would not be able to play in the final if United made it there. United were 2–0 down at the time and looked as though they were heading out of the competition, but even with the knowledge that he would miss out hanging over him, Keane produced one of the best performances of his life to inspire United, so that they overturned that two-goal deficit and won the match 3–2. That showed real mental strength.

Unfortunately for us, Möller seemed to react in the same way in our semi-final at Wembley. He may well have been distraught at the idea of missing the final, but he did not show it. His performance grew and grew in stature and, like Keane, it turned out that he was to play a vital role in the way the game ended.

The Germans got even angrier before the end of normal time when Platty went in high on Sammer. Replays showed he caught him on the knee and, again, in the modern context, with VAR, it might well have been a red card. When everybody watched so much of Euro 96 on television last summer during the lock-down, I think the change in what was punished and what was not punished by referees was one of the most startling things about the footage. Rightly or wrongly, you could get away with a lot more twenty-five years ago.

And so we went to the Golden Goal period of the game. Two minutes in, we should have won it. Platty played a lovely ball through to McManaman and he got to the byline. He looked up and saw Anderton running through the middle in space. He pulled the ball back to him, but Darren hadn't checked his run and the ball went slightly behind him.

Köpke dived for it and missed it. It was just out of his reach.

The goal was gaping. Even though the ball was behind him, Darren still managed to hook it goalwards but it was not the tap-in it might have been and instead of rolling into an empty net, it hit the post and rebounded into the grateful arms of Köpke. It was a huge opportunity missed.

A minute later, Germany might have won it. It was hearts-in-mouths stuff for all of us now. Eilts, who was having a brilliant match in the centre of the German midfield, tapped a pass into the path of Helmer, who was hurtling down the left flank. Helmer lashed the ball across the face of goal with such pace that all it needed was a touch and it would have gone in. Kuntz threw himself headlong at it but it was just too far in front of him. The crowd in the stadium breathed out en masse.

So much for any suggestion that the Golden Goal rule was inhibiting teams. Maybe it had before, but not this evening. Now Möller ran through from the halfway line, driven on by the anger and the vengeance of missing out on the final, playing as if possessed. Tony Adams back-pedalled to buy himself time and allow other defenders to get back and when he got to 25 yards out, Möller let fly. His shot was heading for the top corner, but Dave Seaman arched his back and managed to tip the ball away with his right hand.

Germany swarmed all over us. Möller took an inswinging corner from the right. I went up for it with Gareth and Kuntz. Kuntz just got to it first and the ball went off his head like a bullet. Gazza was on the line but it was too high and too fast for him to do anything apart from stick his hand in the air to try to punch it away. That didn't work and it bulged the roof of the net. For a split second, I thought it was all over, but then I heard the referee's whistle blow. He had seen Kuntz foul Gareth at the corner kick. The goal was ruled out. We were still alive.

Then came the most heart-stopping moment of them all. The most heart-stopping and the most heart-breaking. The moment that we all look back on and think that we were inches away from winning Euro 96. The moment we all look back on and think of the split second that we thought we had beaten Germany. The moment we look back on more than any other and think of what might have been.

We were nine minutes into extra time when Gazza won the ball off Thomas Hässler on the England left. He played it to Anderton, who moved it on to Teddy. Teddy spotted Alan peeling away from Babbel on the right side of the area. He played a ball perfectly into his path and Alan side-footed a volley across goal. It was a cross, not a shot. Alan knew that Gazza was running in at the back post.

I thought we had won it. Everybody thought we had won it. Köpke dived for it and missed and the ball ran on to where Gazza should have been. But there is a consensus about what happened next: Gazza's mind worked too fast. His football brain was too quick. A centre forward who only thought of goals would have followed the path of the ball and tapped it into the net.

But Gazza was not a centre forward. He was always thinking several steps ahead. It was one of the things that made him close to a genius. He saw Shearer's cross and he saw Köpke and he thought Köpke was going to get a touch. So he checked his run in anticipation that Köpke's touch would take the ball straight to him. He hesitated. It was like a glitch on your video. He didn't want to lunge for the ball only to find out that the goalkeeper had deflected it behind him.

Except Köpke didn't get a touch. Alan's cross was too good for him. It eluded him. And that surprised Gazza. He realised too late. He threw himself forward and stuck out his left leg. I don't know if it grazed the studs on the bottom of his boot, but it felt as if he was that close. He lunged, but the ball sailed on and went out for a corner. Gazza ended up over the goal line, but the ball wasn't with him.

I have thought about that moment a lot over the years. What if Gazza had scored? Most of all, I wonder what the reaction would have been if he had scored. And the truth is that I don't think there would ever have been a moment like it at Wembley, except maybe winning the World Cup final. And even that was in a more restrained age.

Gazza is one of the most popular players we have ever had, a larger-than-life figure beloved by the fans. People knew he was vulnerable, people knew how much the game meant to him; they knew that football was everything to him and they also knew that he was our most talented player since Sir Bobby Charlton.

So sometimes I imagine what it would have been like if he had scored in that moment, if he had scored the goal that took us through to our first final in a major tournament for thirty years. Because of the Golden Goal format, there would have been no delay, either. The crowd would have known immediately that we had won the game.

And it was against Germany, too. That was the last element. Gazza would have scored a Golden Goal that had got us to the final of a major tournament and we would have beaten Germany, our greatest rivals, to do it. Every single thing you needed for it to be the ultimate explosion of football joy in this country was there in that one moment.

It is a *Sliding Doors* moment. It was there and then it was gone. If Gazza had scored and we had gone on to win the tournament, what would have happened? Maybe it would have given us the confidence to build on that success. Maybe we would have beaten Argentina in the 1998 World Cup instead of losing to them on penalties. Maybe, instead of always being on the wrong side of fine margins, we would have had the confidence to be on the right side of them.

Gazza actually came close to scoring again a few minutes later. Again, a cross from the right, this time from McManaman, was just too far in front of him. Again, he threw himself at it but couldn't quite reach it. Anderton dragged a shot just wide. It was relentless. Neither team was giving any quarter.

We gathered ourselves for the last fifteen minutes. Christian Ziege came close to getting the winner for them when he ran on to a one-two with Möller. Gareth and I converged on him as he bore down on Seaman, but he got to the ball before us and poked it just wide. It felt like a let-off.

Both teams kept going for it. Incey headed a shot from Marco Bode off the line at one end. At the other, McManaman ran on to a through ball from Shearer, but he was being chased down by Eilts, his shot betrayed his tiredness and Köpke saved it easily.

We had one last half chance. We played a ball towards the box and it bounced up for Platty to head it on towards the penalty spot. Anderton looked like he might get on the end of it, but Eilts, once again, got across to cover and shepherded the ball away to safety. Then the final whistle blew. We were going to penalties against the Germans again.

Both semi-finals against the Germans were great. Whoever was going to win it had to dig deep both times. And even now, I'm glad the games were decided by penalties. I am not one of those who cringes every time there is a penalty shoot-out. I think they are by far the best and most exciting way of finishing a drawn game. That night at Wembley, I didn't think either team deserved to lose the game over two hours of football.

10

GARETH'S TURN

I WASN'T DREADING THE shoot-out. Not at all. I mean, I knew there would be pressure and that it would be horribly nerve-wracking, but I felt we'd get through. We were fresh from the penalty-shoot-out victory against Spain, our takers were in confident mood and Dave Seaman had made the save from Nadal that had won the tie for us in the quarter-final.

So we were ready. We knew the order. Shearer first, Platt second, me third, Gazza fourth and Teddy fifth. If it went beyond that, Gareth and Incey had talked and decided that Gareth would go sixth and Incey seventh. I didn't think it would get that far, partly because of our ability from the spot with our first five, partly because we were in our own stadium in front of our own fans and partly because we had the world's best goalkeeper.

I felt the odds were in our favour. Give me those stats every day. Give me those five takers, give me my goalkeeper, give me home advantage, give me a team that has just won a penalty shoot-out against Spain in a quarter-final. All of a sudden, the chances of victory start stacking up a little bit. I had so much confidence in Dave Seaman. I thought Dave would save at least one. I was positive he would save at least one.

I concentrated on my own task: scoring my penalty. There was no surprise from Terry this time when I said that I wanted to go number three. There was no surprise that I wanted to be part of this and that I wanted the responsibility. What had happened against Spain had convinced him that I needed to be in that line-up and now I had one more ghost to chase away.

My thinking about my own penalty and where to put it was fairly straightforward. I knew the Germans would be as thorough as they could possibly be with their preparations. That was the nature of their professionalism. They wouldn't have left anything to chance. They wouldn't be winging this. They would have thought of all eventualities.

I knew that they had seen us take four penalties against Spain. I knew that Köpke would have studied that shoot-out, as well as all the footage of us from club games he could have got hold of. That's how much I revered the Germans in terms of their preparation. They knew everything there was to know about which way we liked to take penalties.

I knew Shearer and Platty would be taking the first two, so I asked them which way they were going to go. They didn't say. I think either they hadn't decided or they were already in their own bubble by then, focusing on what they had to do, not wanting to give anything away to anybody, not wanting to talk.

As Alan walked up to take the first penalty, I still had no idea whether I was going to whip the ball across my body or side-foot it. I told myself I was going to watch our first two penalties and see how Köpke behaved. I knew which way Alan and Platty had sent their penalties against Spain. I wanted to see if Köpke thought they would go the same way again now.

I wanted to see if he was following a pattern. And if he was following a pattern, then I was going to gamble that he would continue to follow the pattern when I took my penalty. I had no choice but to wait and watch. I stuck to the strategy.

Alan stepped up first. Against Spain, he had hit his penalty high and wide to Zubizarreta's right. This time, he hit it high and wide to Köpke's left. It was a great penalty, but I was watching Köpke. He guessed the other way. He guessed that Alan was going to put it the same side he had put it against Spain.

Thomas Hässler took the first Germany penalty. It was just about perfect. He took a long run-up and lashed the ball low to Dave Seaman's right. It had a lot of power but it was utterly, dispiritingly precise, too. It was right in the corner. Dave went the right way, but he had absolutely no chance.

Platty was next up for us. He had gone to Zubizarreta's left against Spain. He ran up and put it the same way. I saw the ball hit the back of the net and my heart leapt again, but I had my eyes fixed on Köpke. He had guessed correctly this time. He had guessed that Platty would go the same way he had against Spain.

So my mind was made up. Maybe mathematicians and statisticians would query the wisdom of identifying a pattern based on only two events, but it was all I had. I told myself that Köpke had seen me whip the ball across my body against Spain and go to the keeper's left. I told myself that he would guess I was going the same way again.

I still had to wait. Thomas Strunz, who had come on two minutes before the end of extra time as a substitute for Steffen Freund, took Germany's second penalty. Strunz hit it high to Seaman's right and it sped into the roof of the net. Like Hässler's, it was as close as you can get to the perfect penalty. The best goalkeeper in the world didn't get anywhere near it.

So now it was my turn. I had to keep my nerve and stick with my strategy. The worst thing is changing your mind on the long walk to the penalty spot. Never change your mind. Never let doubt enter your head. That is death to penalty-takers. That is when you are in trouble. Never change your mind. Never change your mind.

Köpke had anticipated that Shearer and Platt would go the same way they had against Spain. One of them went the same way, one changed. The thought occurred to me that Köpke must know that I knew he had gone the same way the first two takers had gone against Spain. He knew that I knew, so maybe he would change his strategy this time. That was the only element of doubt in my mind. It was possible he was setting me up. Like a bowler bowling a few outswingers in succession at a batsman and then getting one to nip back off the seam. It was a game of bluff and double-bluff. But even before Strunz had taken his penalty, I had decided I was sticking with Plan A.

I walked to the spot and I did not waver. I was not going to whip it across my body this time. I was going to side-foot it into the opposite corner. I knew I would be sacrificing some of the power I could get by going the other way, but I was banking on the fact that it wouldn't matter because Köpke would have gone the wrong way. That was the gamble.

I couldn't change that now. So I just told myself, 'All I have to do is change sides and I'll score.' And that's what happened. Köpke gambled on me whipping the ball across my body. He went to his left and I put it to his right. It wasn't a great penalty. It was only the fact that I managed to second-guess the goalkeeper that saved me. If he had guessed the right way, he would have saved it.

I've seen enough penalties saved to know it was of a nice height for a goalkeeper. If he had dived the right way, he would have beaten it away with his hands. It was probably no better than Gareth's penalty, which was a couple of minutes away. It was just that, in my case, the goalie went the other way and all of a sudden it looked like a better penalty than it actually was.

I had done my preparation. I had thought it out. It would have been easy for me to step up and whip it across my body again because that was the penalty I was most comfortable with psychologically. It was a struggle with my mentality to say I was going to change sides. But I stuck with the plan and it paid off. I was just relying on a German being a German and being thorough. And Köpke didn't let me down.

My job was done. I didn't let the emotions out in quite the same way I had against Spain. I suppose I'd got that out of my system. This time, I settled for what one commentator described as 'a modest thumbs-up'. I was relieved, obviously. I was elated, too. I still believed we were going to win. I still believed in our penalty-takers and I still believed Dave was going to get to one of their kicks. Nothing had changed.

As I walked back to the centre circle, I saw Stefan Reuter coming in the other direction. Reuter had had a fine game but he looked tired. I also remembered that he had picked up a second yellow card during the match, so he wouldn't be playing in the final if Germany got there. I wondered if it might have affected him just a little. I wondered if this would be our chance.

He ran up and struck his penalty well, but Dave Seaman guessed correctly and went to his left. It was the weakest of the three Germany penalties so far and Dave got his fingertips to it. But he couldn't keep it out. His touch pushed it into the roof of the net and made it look better than it was. The reality was that it was our first sniff of an opportunity in the shoot-out and it had gone. Dave swiped at the turf in frustration.

Gazza took our fourth penalty. Please don't miss. Not Gazza. I needn't have worried. He went to the keeper's right against Spain, but this time he went to the keeper's left and, once again, his penalty was beautifully precise. Just inside the post. Köpke stuck to his plan and guessed Gazza was going to put it the same way he had put it against Spain.

Christian Ziege was next for them. Would this be it? Would this be the moment one of them cracked? Do Germans ever crack? Incey was sitting in the centre circle, facing the other way. He couldn't even watch. Ziege put it high to Dave Seaman's left. Dave went the right away again, but this time the penalty was too good and he couldn't get close to it. It was 4–4. Now it was sudden death.

Teddy was the next one to walk the long walk. 'It must have been the most nervous I'd ever been on a football pitch,' he said later. 'You know that if you miss, you're going to be remembered for it.' I knew that as well as anybody. But Teddy didn't betray any of those nerves that were coursing through him.

He hadn't taken a penalty against Spain because he had been substituted before the end of extra time. Robbie Fowler replaced him in the game and would have replaced him in the penalty line-up, too. Robbie was down for the fifth pen against Spain, but Teddy didn't have any doubts about stepping up this time. He probably had the best football technique of anyone in the squad apart from Gazza.

He ran up and put the ball high to Köpke's left. He may have been nervous but it looked like a nerveless penalty. Köpke guessed the wrong way but it wouldn't have mattered if he had guessed the right way. He still wouldn't have got anywhere near it. It flew into the roof of the net. The standard of penalties from both sides had been amazing.

So if Germany missed now, we were through. Kuntz walked up to take the fifth penalty. Now that is pressure. He had scored Germany's goal with his right foot, but he took the penalty with his favoured left foot. The stadium held its breath. The tension inside Wembley was almost unbearable. We were so close. Closer to a final than at any time since 1966.

Kuntz strode up and hit one of the best penalties I have ever seen. He put it in pretty much the same spot where Teddy had put his a few seconds earlier. High in the corner. Dave had no chance. Zero. To do that in those circumstances with everything on the line was unbelievable. He trusted his technique, he trusted all his hours of practice and he got on with it. It was 5–5.

I looked round and saw Gareth starting to walk towards the spot. Gareth was my closest friend in the team. I knew he wasn't a regular penalty-taker, but it wasn't a surprise to me that he had put his hand up and taken responsibility. That was Gareth all over. Even in a situation like this, where there was so much on the line, he was putting his head above the parapet.

If things went pear-shaped at any of the clubs he was at throughout his career, before and after Euro 96, it was always Gareth in front of the media. It became a standing joke between us. If things were going well at Villa or Middlesbrough, you never saw Gareth. All the other players would come out to take the credit and do the easy interviews about how well they were playing. As soon as things started going wrong, everyone else ducked for cover and the press officer would turn to Gareth because they knew he would front up. He was the man for the crisis. He was the player who never ducked a challenge. When the going got tough, it would always be Gareth standing there in front of the bright lights.

That is one of the reasons I find it so refreshing to have him as England manager now. It's one of a multitude of reasons. The football is good. It's kind on the eye. And we are getting results. That's obviously really important. But we have got a fella in there who is in it for everybody else. Not just himself. He does what is best for the long term as well as trying to achieve results in the short term.

He has always had a mentality to push through the younger players. The importance of the younger generation in the age-group England sides being successful is a big thing for him. I always made decisions that were beneficial for the players and not myself when I was with the England Under-21s, and he did the same. He does the same with the senior side now.

If I called a player up from the Under-20s or the Under-19s, I wouldn't do it at the cost of him getting ninety minutes' football. I'd put him in my Under-21s starting line-up. Otherwise, it's not fair to him. It's counter-productive. It's robbing him of valuable development time.

I have seen too many managers, especially at senior level, pick a squad and be oblivious to the impact that it may have on a player's career. A case in point is when Theo Walcott was picked to go to the World Cup in 2006 and he never kicked a ball. I don't think we qualified for the Under-21 tournament that summer, but it was still counter-productive taking him to Germany. It did nothing for him except raise expectation levels to an absurd degree. It was done by a manager who had no fore-thought about the implications it would have on the player. Great, he went to a World Cup at the age of 12, or whatever it was, but he didn't kick a ball.

Theo is a good example of a player whose international career has been mismanaged by the Football Association. If Gareth, or I, had been in charge of the England senior team back then, he wouldn't have been treated like that. When Gareth was Under-21 manager, he looked after the players for whom he had respon-sibility. He gave help and guidance to the coaches below him. Those are all things that stem from the fact that he is unselfish. That's what Gareth is – and I like to think that is how I was in the job, too, and maybe that's why I sometimes wasn't cut out to be a manager.

Another reason I wasn't surprised to see Gareth walking towards that penalty spot is that people have underestimated his toughness. If you balance up me and Gareth, people overesti-mate my toughness and underestimate his. That's because of the public perception of the way we are on a football pitch. If I tell someone I'm going to the theatre, they look at me and say, 'Are you OK, what's happened to you?' I'm not quite what people think I am from what they see on the pitch. And neither is Gareth. If you are in the public eye and you do a job that is very visual, people think they know your personality. But if they think Gareth is a soft touch in some way, they're wrong. You underestimate Gareth at your cost.

To stay in management at the level he has, to be as successful as he has been, you have to be hard-nosed. He knows what is right and what is wrong both in life and in professional football. He will make tough calls. Look at Joe Hart. It would have been easy to take Joe to the World Cup in 2018. I would have done. But Gareth did the tough thing and backed his judgement.

I'm not sure if I knew that the man I played alongside at Euro 96 was going to be a successful manager back then. I mean, I knew he had excellent qualities, but I still can't look at a player even now and say with any degree of certainty whether he is going to be a successful manager. I don't know what it takes to be a successful manager. You need a big stroke of luck somewhere along the line, for a start.

Gareth has great man-management skills and you need those more than ever these days. That's one of the main things that make him a good manager in today's society. Your man-management has got to be better than your football knowledge in some ways. You have to be adaptable. You have to accept that ways of behaviour have changed. You have to accept that the power lies in different places in the game.

I think people sense that Gareth has their interests at heart. You can't fake that. Players pick up on that, the way schoolkids sense it in a teacher. He puts the group before himself. There is nobody in the modern game as unselfish as him. He was liked across the board as a player and now it is the same as a coach and manager, whether it is by the media or players. If results took a turn for the worse and he thought falling on his own sword would make England successful, he would do it.

You might not think it, but I'm quite like Gareth in some ways. All right, Gareth doesn't beat his chest on a football pitch, but one of the things we have got in common is that we share the same philosophy of representing our country. I sat and talked with Gareth for an hour at St George's Park before Christmas 2019 and we chatted about our philosophies. We are so similar in what we feel is right for the England national team.

We took the same route in management to an extent, too. In my case, Manchester City offered me a job at the end of my playing career, I took it and I was fire-fighting from day one. Gareth followed a similar path at Middlesbrough. When I was England Under-21 manager, I used to do club visits and I went to Middlesbrough and when I was there, I told Gareth he needed a job like mine.

He needed a chance to breathe. He needed a chance to impose his ideas and his character on a job rather than be stuck in one long spell of crisis management. A year later, when I moved on, Gareth was appointed to the England Under-21 role and it was ideal for him. It's more than just a job to him. I think people can see that. That's one of the reasons I like him. He cares about the whole situation. He cares about the people he manages and the people around him.

One of his biggest achievements is that he won the media over. Every England manager that I have worked under or worked with or just observed has failed to do that. Suddenly there has been an outbreak of empathy. Maybe the media have met the England manager halfway and they are a bit more forgiving, but Gareth has to take great credit.

The open day that he and the FA staged before the World Cup in 2018, where every player was made available to the media and things were not as tightly controlled as before, was a revolution in media relations between the media and the England team, but it was also a master stroke. I think the players benefited from it as well.

In the past, they had been closed off and suspicious. I don't blame them for that one bit. How could I? That was always the way I was. I never gave anything to the media. But Gareth persuaded them that they ought to talk and that they ought to tell their stories, because some of them have amazing stories about how they got here and what they have been through. The players trusted him and they told their stories and the public loved their stories.

Gareth has always been someone who inspires trust and as he walked up to that penalty spot, I was confident he was going to score. But I also knew that once you get to the scenario of sudden death, you always have your heart in your mouth. You are one piece of bad luck or bad judgement away from elimination.

I don't like calling penalty shoot-outs a 'lottery'. There is way more to them than that. But there are elements you can't control and perhaps the biggest of those is that you can't be sure of predicting how the opposition perform and how good or bad their penalties are going to be. That's out of your hands.

In my wildest dreams, I had never thought Dave Seaman would be beaten five times in a row, but by the time Gareth walked up to the spot, that was what had happened. In the end, you have to hold your hands up and say well done. You admire the Germans for what they have done. You admire them for being calm under pressure away from home as well.

Don't forget that they had been under additional pressure all the way through the shoot-out, because they were the team going second. The more penalties we scored without missing, the greater the pressure on them. But they kept responding with superb penalties. They kept dealing with that. And in the end, the pressure got to us instead.

Gareth put the ball down, took a few steps back and started his run-up. He hit the ball low and to the goalkeeper's right. Köpke guessed correctly. He dived low and got his body and his hands behind the ball. He pushed it out. Gareth stopped dead and put his hands on his hips and stared down at the floor.

I knew what he was going through. I could say that honestly. I walked a few steps out of the centre circle to go to meet him and console him as we waited for Andy Möller to take the final penalty. I knew it was over. I knew Möller wasn't going to miss. The only time the pressure was relieved on them was when Gareth missed. It was a free shot for them now.

Möller ran up and hit the ball as hard as he could. It was another brilliant penalty. It went past Dave before he had time to move and smashed into the roof of the net. Möller set off for the area behind the goal and hitched his shorts up in some sort of bizarre celebration that was supposed to be an imitation of Gazza, I think. Good luck to him.

There was a strange finality about that moment. One second, all your hopes are still alive and it feels as if there is so much ahead of you. It feels as if there are so many possibilities and that there is no world beyond the tournament you are playing in. There is no world beyond the rest of the squad and the team-mates you are existing with at the hotel and on the coach and on the pitch.

It is a time when all your sensibilities are heightened and you are aware you are living through something special, something that only comes along once or twice in a career. You are in the bubble and there is nothing outside the bubble. And then a German goalkeeper saves a penalty and a German midfielder scores a penalty and the bubble bursts and the outside world comes flooding back in.

It is that sudden. We were out of the tournament. I was out of the tournament. I thought it was the last time I would ever wear an England shirt. I thought it was the last time I would ever look up at the stands from the pitch at Wembley. I knew beforehand it was either going to be the happiest day of my life or the worst, and all of those things conspired in one second to make it the worst.

I walked around the pitch and started crying because I thought it was my last time, and that was as bad as anything because of what it meant to me to be an England international. I was in a daze, really. I even swapped shirts with Hässler, even though I preferred not doing that. I had a lot of respect for Hässler. On this occasion, it felt like the right thing to do.

It was a horrible feeling walking around Wembley. When Köpke saved Gareth's penalty, it was almost like a stab in the heart to me. If we had beaten Germany, we really felt we would have gone on and won it all. But now it was just another semi-final defeat. I played three tournaments and two of them ended with semi-final defeats to Germany on penalties.

When I got back to the dressing room, it was quiet. I did my best to console Gareth but I knew that sometimes all you want is to be left alone. He sat with assistant coach Bryan Robson for a while and in the end I think he went up to do media. Just like Gareth. Still refusing to duck it even then. Still fronting up when all he really wanted was to be allowed to mourn for what had slipped away from us.

When we were all back on the coach, I asked Terry if I could have the microphone for a minute to talk to the lads. I like to draw a line under things and I told them I had just played my last game for England and that I was retiring from international football. 'Don't worry, though,' I said, 'I'll still be around in the league next season to kick the **** out of all of you.'

And then I sat there in the silence and tried to come to terms with what had just happened on the pitch. You get institutionalised at a tournament, and then in that one final moment all your camaraderie is taken away from you. All that you were trying to achieve is stripped away. It sounds selfish, but if you have put your life into trying to be the best footballer you can be, you feel lost when it is over.

My God, it's a soulless feeling. It's an incredible feeling of anticlimax. I know some players who go to tournaments and miss their home and hate being locked away. I've never been like that. Being with that group of players, with Gazza and Tony Adams and Gareth and so many footballers I admired, and trying to win that tournament in front of our own fans felt like living life to the limit.

We didn't win, but we were part of something special. We

were part of a moment when the country came together – and we were at the heart of it. We were at the heart of trying to end those thirty years of hurt, and now we were driving back to Burnham Beeches in silence and all the flags had gone and no one was singing 'Three lions on a shirt' any more.

It was over and it was a killer.

11

THE EXORCISTS

IT TURNED OUT the game against Germany wasn't the last time I played for England after all, despite my little speech on the coach at Wembley. When Glenn Hoddle took over from Terry Venables, he asked me if I would reconsider my decision to retire. I didn't have to think about it for too long. Playing for England was always the biggest honour in my career.

I played eight more times for my country after Euro 96. I played in our first game after the tournament, a World Cup qualifier against Moldova in Chișinău in September 1996, and the match against Italy at Wembley the following February, when we lost to a fine goal from Gianfranco Zola.

I missed out on the 1998 World Cup, but when Kevin Keegan succeeded Glenn, he picked me for a couple of games, too. I made my seventy-eighth and final England appearance in a European Championship qualifier against Poland in Warsaw on 8 September 1999. It was a 0–0 draw.

I was 37 years and 136 days old that night in Poland. I was the third oldest outfield player ever to have represented England, behind Stanley Matthews and Leslie Compton. I was proud of that. I like to think the desire that I had to play for my country fuelled my longevity.

*   *   *

The pain of losing in the semi-final at Euro 96 eventually faded away. I remember it now as the best football experience of my life. It was the best playing environment that I had ever been a part of.

In the aftermath of the tournament, I was even able to salvage a bit of humour from our exit. Pizza Hut offered me, Chris Waddle and Gareth a decent fee if we would take part in an advert for them that centred around the theme of those of us who had missed penalties for England in shoot-outs.

After Turin, I don't think I would have done it. It would still have been too raw. But by now, I had things in perspective. Gareth took a bit more persuading because the pain of what had happened to him was still fresh, but he agreed in the end. It was cathartic for us to be able to laugh at ourselves.

It starts off with me and Chris sitting in a Pizza Hut restaurant with Gareth, who has a brown paper bag over his head so nobody can recognise him. The waitress walks past and I shout, 'Miss, miss.' She gives us the pizzas. 'Come on, Gareth,' I say, 'it only took me six years to get over it.'

Gareth takes the bag off his head and has a bite of the pizza. 'Thanks a lot, boys,' he says, 'I feel much better now.' He gets up and walks over to get something and bangs straight into another part of the restaurant. 'This time he's hit the post,' I say, and Chris and I burst into a fit of giggles.

No one's laughing at Gareth any more. He recovered from the trauma of that night at Wembley and enjoyed the rest of a fine playing career before he went into management. He continued to earn the respect of all those around him with the honesty and dignity with which he conducted himself.

And in 2018, he emulated my two bosses in 1990 and 1996,

Sir Bobby Robson and Terry Venables, by leading England to the semi-finals of a major tournament. England fell to Croatia in that last-four match in Moscow in 2018, but Gareth proved to everyone what I already knew: he is the kind of leader you can like and admire.

I enjoyed the rest of my playing career, too. I started picking up more injuries, which happens as you get older. When I was at West Ham, I even managed to add to my reputation for toughness by attempting to run off a broken leg.

Actually, I broke my leg twice in one season at West Ham. I'd played eight games for them at the start of the 1999–2000 season when I went into a tackle with Micah Hyde during a game against Watford at Upton Park. No complaints about the tackle. It was a fair challenge.

I heard a crack but I just thought that my shin pad had broken. I had a bit of treatment and walked to the side of the pitch. My leg was sore, but it was right on the brink of half-time. Harry Redknapp was the West Ham boss and he told me to go back to the dressing room so he could see how I was during the interval.

I went into the dressing room and got on the treatment couch and iced my shin and Harry came in and asked how I was doing and I said I thought it was all right. 'It should be OK,' I said. 'Let me give it a run.' I got off the bed and walked over to the corridor by the tunnel. I tried to run and, my God, it was sore. I said, 'Harry, I'm no good.'

I had an X-ray and it showed the tackle had cracked my shin bone near enough all the way through. There was just a little bit hanging on, so if I had gone back out, I would have shredded my tibia and fibula in the first challenge.

Five months later I came back and played against Southampton in my second game back. Kevin Davies was running in the opposite direction to me and his kneecap hit me straight on the point where I had broken my shin bone and it went again. I walked off.

I knew I had broken my shin, but I walked round the side of the pitch with the help of the physios. The old instincts had kicked in: don't show vulnerability in anything you do. The way my old man taught me, stuff like that was non-negotiable. If you got hurt, you got up.

Penalties remained part of my story, too. When I played my last club game, for Manchester City against Portsmouth at Maine Road on 21 April 2002, I only needed one more goal to complete 100 goals over the course of my career and Kevin Keegan, the City manager, said that I could take all the set pieces and any penalties we got.

There was already a celebratory atmosphere at the game anyway, because we had won the Division One championship and were heading back to the Premier League. I was the skipper and City needed four goals to reach 109 for the season and break their all-time club record. I set up a goal for Steve Howey early on and deep into the second half, we were leading 3–1.

Sure enough, we were awarded a penalty in the ninety-fifth minute of the match and I stepped up to take it. Dave Beasant was the Pompey keeper and we had had a laugh before the start about how he'd let me roll the ball into the net if I got a penalty. I should have listened to him. I decided to blast it instead and I put it over the crossbar.

When I became a manager, it was hardly a surprise, given my history, that I should make penalty shoot-outs a particular speciality of mine. I was manager of the England Under-21s from 2007 to 2013 and in that period I would bet that we were the best-prepared team in the world when it came to shoot-outs.

In the build-up to the Under-21 European Championship in Sweden in 2009, we practised penalties after every training session. This was two years away from the tournament. We never had a training session without the players sitting on the halfway line, then walking to take a penalty and that being recorded on film, to add to our collection of every penalty they had ever taken for their club.

We recorded hundreds of penalties. We had a huge database of information. That is preparation. If you only start thinking about it the day before a major tournament, that's no good to man nor beast. It's a waste of time. It's a waste of time because the manager does not know who his best five penalty-takers are or in what order those potential penalty-takers should be.

Too many managers in the past have been blinkered to that. They have effectively surrendered before a ball has been kicked. They have said it's just a lottery. I think that's bad management. Nobody would say, 'It's just a lottery, so we don't practise corners,' or 'It's just a lottery, so David Beckham needn't practise a thousand free kicks.' There has been an abdication of responsibility for preparing teams for penalty shoot-outs over the years. There is a duty to prepare as much as you can to reduce the element of chance that you have to accept is always going to play some part in a shoot-out.

At the far end of the lottery scale is taking a person off the street and asking him to take a penalty. They might score. They might not. That is totally random. As a manager and ex-player, I wanted to bring the lottery scale down as low as I possibly could. You will never get it down to nought. You can never get a situation where you are guaranteed to get a penalty all the time. Probably the best penalty-taker there has ever been in the Premier League, James Milner, will miss a penalty on occasion.

When our semi-final against Sweden in the 2009 European Under-21 Championship went to penalties, James slipped just as he was taking our first and he sliced the ball well wide. It happens. It is impossible to legislate for that kind of thing. But the fact remains that too many non-penalty-taking players have missed penalties in critical shoot-outs for it to be just random.

The good penalty-takers, the takers that you know are good, stand up and take penalties and they score more than they miss. And I have done the practice with poor penalty-takers over the years and they still missed. There are good and bad penalty-takers. Players are better at some aspects of the game than they are at others.

When we made an exhaustive study of penalty-taking before those Under-21 Euros, the lowest scoring ratio for any player we had was over 50 per cent anyway. Even a nugget of a footballer will score one in two. An idiot. But in a shoot-out in an elite competition, that's no good.

We are talking the fine details here, but it can be the difference between a player who is at the back end of 80 per cent and one who is around 70 per cent that knocks you out of a major tournament. It is about giving yourself the best chance. Some people still don't want to do the preparation to find out what the percentages are for each individual player who will ever wear an international jersey, and I think that's lazy.

My mentality when I joined the FA – and what I tried to put into practice – was that as soon as a young player comes into the English system, he should practise penalties at every age group. So say the Victory Shield, Under-16s, after every training session, they take a penalty and it is recorded and logged and they practise right the way through.

Hopefully, by the time they have had a career that gets them on the senior international stage, you will have a back catalogue of hundreds of penalties practised by that individual, so you know full well you can feed back to them which their best penalty is and which way to take it. They will also have had hours of practice and you will know your 80 percenters without even thinking about it.

An England senior manager now probably won't have to do as much research, because by the time players have got to the senior team you have a multitude of stats that can back up your selection, and that is my vision of how England from the penalty spot should always be.

At Euro 96, ask me now who should have gone number six instead of Gareth that night against Germany and I'll tell you I don't know. And I think that proves my point. I don't know what Paul Ince was like from the spot, I don't know how good he or Tony Adams or Dave Seaman were at penalties. I have no idea. I would be guessing, like you. You would be asking me to pluck a name out of six. I rest my case.

If you are going round before a shoot-out asking for volunteers, you've got it wrong. If I saw that, I'd know you'd got it wrong. In any team I have managed, there would be no volunteers for penalties. It would be on statistics alone. I'm not interested in hunches or whether you think someone has a nice technique, or if they've scored a lot of goals from normal play or if they say they're confident. I want to see the stats. And I will trust the stats.

I don't want to speak ill of Fabrice Muamba. He was a fine player and I picked him in the England Under-21 squad for that 2009 European Championship in Sweden. He is also probably one of the worst strikers of the ball I have ever seen and could not hit a cow's arse with a banjo, but statistically he scored more often with his penalties than classic penalty-takers.

It was hard to believe, but statistics do not lie and that is what the statistics said. If you did not do the analysis, you would not know. He just had a knack of scoring. If you didn't analyse the practice, you wouldn't know. He would kick the floor first and it would still go in. He would scuff one and it would go in. It was unbelievable.

I had a massive stand-up argument with Steve Wigley, who was my assistant with England, as we were about to go into that tournament when I told him that if we got past the fifth taker, the next best was Fabrice Muamba. He said that if I put him up to take a penalty, he was quitting the game. He said Fabrice couldn't strike the ball. He said he slapped it.

So I asked Steve why we had bothered doing the stats for the past two years if we were going to ignore them when it really mattered, because of a gut feeling. That's probably how two different coaches end up having a different mentality. My mentality would be to back the stats every day. His mentality was a gut reaction that we couldn't put him up to take a penalty because he hasn't got a goalscoring record and he is useless at kicking the ball.

So take your pick. I'd go with the *Moneyball* stats analysis every time. Why go to the effort of all those years of analysis and then, when it comes to it, ignore it all? If the stats were equal or marginal, I'd err on the side of my gut feeling. I'd take into account the fact a player had had a good game and had his tail up and that sort of thing. But I certainly wouldn't override the stats by 5 per cent. No way. Muamba didn't end up taking one in Sweden, because he was substituted before the end of extra time in that semi-final, but he would have taken the sixth if he had still been on the pitch at the end.

The other thing the analysis taught me was that if a goal-keeper is good at taking penalties in training, trust him in the real thing. Goalkeepers are often bloody good penalty-takers. They are usually decent strikers of the ball and they also know what goalkeepers don't like. Most of them will come up and drive a ball and drive it well. I don't see many keepers step up and not put a bit of power behind it. They tend to hit it as hard as they possibly can and say, 'Try and stop that.'

And if you are talking about pressure, you almost take the pressure off the goalkeeper when he is taking the penalty, because less is expected of him. It's almost as if you are introducing a comic turn. There is less pressure on the goalkeeper than there is on an outfield player.

So in Sweden, after James Milner had missed our first penalty, Joe Hart took our second. The stats showed he was quite clearly one of our top-five penalty-takers, so there was no way I was going to override them. I knew that if we missed a second penalty, the odds would be stacked heavily against us, but you have to trust the stats.

Joe took the penalty and it was one of the best penalties I have seen in tournament conditions. Think the Germany penalties in Euro 96 and it was as good as them. He hit it hard and he hit it high and it smashed into the roof of the net and the Sweden goalkeeper didn't have a chance.

We missed our first penalty that day, our goalkeeper scored our second, Adam Johnson, who we had brought on a few minutes from the end of extra time because he was one of our best takers, scored with aplomb, too, and we ended up winning the shoot-out 5–4.

We went through to a major final on a penalty shoot-out with me as the manager. In 2018, Gareth led England into a World Cup second-round match against Colombia and that went to penalties. Eric Dier scored the winning penalty. It was the first time England had ever won a penalty shoot-out at a World Cup.

And so in our own ways, Gareth and I exorcised more of our ghosts. I'd already got rid of most of mine with those penalties against Spain and Germany at Wembley, but we still lost the shoot-out to Germany. Beating Sweden and then seeing Gareth's England beat Colombia, seeing how much of a difference planning and practice made, banishing the lazy idea that it was all just a lottery, ridding ourselves of the notion that England players lacked the technique or the balls for a shoot-out – it felt like a vindication that had been a long time coming.

PHOTOGRAPHIC ACKNOWLEDGEMENTS

The author and publisher would like to thank the following for permission to reproduce photographs:

Section One: Phil Cole/Getty Images; Jim Hutchison/*Daily Mail*/Shutterstock; Bob Thomas Sports Photography via Getty Images; Bob Thomas Sports Photography via Getty Images; Colorsport/Shutterstock; Juha Tamminen/AFLO/PA Images; Simon Bruty/Allsport/Getty Images; Bob Thomas Sports Photography via Getty Images; Ross Kinnaird/EMPICS Sport; David Giles/PA Archive/PA Images; Allstar Picture Library Ltd/Alamy Stock Photo; Adam Butler/PA Archive/PA Images; Popperfoto via Getty Images/Getty Images; Action Images/Reuters; Ben Radford/Allsport/Getty Images; Colorsport/Shutterstock; Professional Sport/Popperfoto via Getty Images; Ted Blackbrow/Associated Newspapers/Shutterstock; Daniel Bardou/Onze/Icon Sport/Getty Images; Action Images/Reuters; Neal Simpson/EMPICS Sport; Neal Simpson/EMPICS Sport.

Section Two: Bob Thomas Sports Photography via Getty Images; Laurence Griffiths/EMPICS Sport; Colorsport/Shutterstock; Ben Radford/Allsport/Getty Images; Laurence Griffiths/EMPICS Sport; Paul Grover/*The Telegraph*; Popperfoto via Getty Images; Mirrorpix/Reach Licensing; Laurence Griffiths/EMPICS Sport; Colorsport/Shutterstock; Bob Thomas Sports Photography via Getty Images; Bob Thomas Sports Photography via Getty Images; Laurence Griffiths/EMPICS Sport; Action Images/Reuters; Stu Forster/Allsport/Getty Images/Hulton Archive; Bob Thomas Sports Photography via Getty Images; Phil Cole/Getty Images; Laurence Griffiths/Getty Images; Reuters/Kai Pfaffenbach.

Every reasonable effort has been made to trace the copyright holders, but if there are any errors or omissions, Hodder & Stoughton will be pleased to insert the appropriate acknowledgement in any subsequent printings or editions.

INDEX